The Asperger
Couple's Workbook

by the same author
Aspergers in Love
Maxine Aston
Foreword by Gisela Slater-Walker
ISBN 978 1 84310 115 4
eISBN 978 1 84642 394 9

of related interest
Alone Together
Making an Asperger Marriage Work
Katrin Bentley
Foreword by Tony Attwood
ISBN 978 1 84310 537 4
eISBN 978 1 84642 623 0

Love, Sex and Long-Term Relationships
What People with Asperger Syndrome Really Really Want
Sarah Hendrickx
Foreword by Stephen M. Shore
ISBN 978 1 84310 605 0
eISBN 978 1 84642 764 0

Asperger Syndrome and Alcohol
Drinking to Cope?
Matthew Tinsley and Sarah Hendrickx
Foreword by Temple Grandin
ISBN 978 1 84310 609 8
eISBN 978 1 84642 814 2

Autistics' Guide to Dating
A Book by Autistics, for Autistics and Those Who Love Them
or Who Are in Love with Them
Emilia Murry Ramey and Jody John Ramey
ISBN 978 1 84310 881 8
eISBN 978 1 84642 763 3

Asperger Meets Girl
Happy Endings for Asperger Boys
Jonathan Griffiths
Foreword by Hugh Jones
ISBN 978 1 84310 630 2
eISBN 978 1 84642 756 5

The Asperger Couple's Workbook

Practical Advice and Activities for Couples and Counsellors

MAXINE ASTON

FOREWORD BY TONY ATTWOOD

Illustrations by
ANTONY CORBETT
and WILLIAM ASTON

Jessica Kingsley *Publishers*
London and Philadelphia

First published in 2009
by Jessica Kingsley Publishers
73 Collier Street
London N1 9BE, UK
and
400 Market Street, Suite 400
Philadelphia, PA 19106, USA

www.jkp.com

Library of Congress Cataloging in Publication Data
Aston, Maxine C.
 The Asperger couple's workbook : practical advice and activities for couples and counsellors / Maxine
Aston.
   p. cm.
 Includes bibliographical references.
 ISBN 978-1-84310-253-3 (pb : alk. paper)
 1. Asperger's syndrome–Patients–Family relationships. 2. Asperger's syndrome–Patients–
Rehabilitation. 3. Interpersonal communication. 4. Marital psychotherapy. I. Title.
 RC553.A88A4883 2009
 616.85'8832–dc22

                            2008019376

British Library Cataloguing in Publication Data
A CIP catalogue record for this book is available from the British Library

ISBN 978 1 84310 253 3
eISBN 978 1 84642 851 7

Printed and bound in Great Britain

For Duckk (Quack)

Difference can only feel threatening if it exists in the absence of acceptance and understanding.

Maxine Aston (2008)

CONTENTS

Chapter One
Understanding the Difference 15

The different species concept; Different needs; A different way of
thought processing; A different perspective

Chapter Two
Communication 23

Communicating on different wavelengths; One thing at a time;
Rules for giving important messages; Memory aids; Expressing
feelings; Feelings in colour; The card communication system;
Three rules for good arguing; Strategies to avoid breaking the
rules; The frustration or anger thermometer; Whole sentence
strategy; Unresolved issues

Chapter Three
Non-verbal Communication 53

Assumptions; Intonation of communication; MAD moments

Chapter Four
Social Interaction. 61

Important socialising rules; A need for a different environment;
Celebrations; Arranging surprise celebrations; Getting the
context right

FOREWORD

There are people who easily fall in love with someone who has Asperger's syndrome because of the positive attributes of the syndrome. The person can be extraordinarily attentive, very knowledgeable, kind, slightly immature, physically attractive, quiet, and inexperienced in relationships. There can be compassion for the person's limited social understanding and for their having been the victim of teasing and bullying. The partner with Asperger's syndrome is often appreciated for being confident about opinions, predictable and honest. In the very early stages of the relationship, these positive characteristics are very appealing and love is blind. Gradually, often over many years, there may be a recognition of some of the more negative attributes, and a realization that the relationship is not what was expected.

The person with Asperger's syndrome can fall in love with someone who has exceptional social understanding and empathy for his or her difficulties; as one partner said regarding her husband who has Asperger's syndrome, 'I saw the heart, not the behaviour'. The person with Asperger's syndrome appreciates not being criticised for being socially naive or clumsy, and being guided in social situations by someone who understands the confusion and exhaustion associated with socializing. The non-Asperger's syndrome partner is prepared to be an 'executive secretary' to help with organizational problems, and continue many of the emotional support functions previously provided by a parent. However, after several years of living together, the relationship may not be as originally expected for the partner with Asperger's syndrome.

The courtship usually does not provide an indication of the problems that can develop later in the relationship. The person with Asperger's syndrome may have developed a superficial expertise in the early stages of a relationship, especially in romance and dating from watching television programs and films, and from mimicking the 'script' of the actors or their romantic gestures, such as bringing flowers. For the non-Asperger's syndrome partner, what was endearing at the start of the relationship later becomes a problem. The initial optimism that his or her partner will gradually change and become more emotionally mature and socially skilled, can dissolve into despair that social skills are static due to limited motivation to be more sociable. The person with Asperger's syndrome needs periods of social isolation at home, and joint social contact with friends and family can slowly diminish. The non-Asperger's syndrome partner may reluctantly agree to reduce the frequency and duration of social contact for the sake of the relationship, gradually absorbing the characteristics of Asperger's syndrome into their own personality. A partner said to me, 'The essential me had disappeared.'

A significant problem for the non-Asperger's syndrome partner is feeling lonely. The partner with Asperger's syndrome can be content with his or her own company for long periods of time. Conversations may be superficial, and from the perspective of the partner with Asperger's syndrome, primarily an exchange of information rather than an enjoyment of each other's company, experiences and shared opinions. A man with Asperger's syndrome said, 'My pleasure doesn't come from an emotional or interpersonal exchange.' There is the expectation in a relationship of regular expressions of love and affection. What may be missing in the relationship are daily words and gestures of affection. The non-Asperger's syndrome partner can feel affection deprivation, which can be a contributory factor to low self-esteem and a clinical depression.

The partner with Asperger's syndrome can feel that whatever he or she says or does cannot make their partner feel happy. They unintentionally keep getting it wrong and feel excessively criticized. They may begin to believe that sometimes it is wiser to do or say nothing. Access to survival strategies, such as solitude and the special interest, can become restricted, especially with the arrival of children. The relationship is deteriorating but the partner with Asperger's syndrome can be unaware of why and what to do.

This workbook was written by Maxine Aston to provide insight into the perspectives of each partner and to give practical advice and suggest constructive activities to strengthen the relationship. Maxine has considerable experience as a relationship counsellor specializing in couples where one or both partners have the distinct characteristics of Asperger's syndrome. The suggestions are simple and effective. If the reader is in such a relationship, and unable to benefit from relationship counselling with a specialist counsellor, then this workbook is an excellent starting point. Relationship counsellors will also benefit from the explanations and activities, as their client base will undoubtedly include couples where one or both partners have the characteristics associated with Asperger's syndrome.

— *Professor Tony Attwood,*
author of The Complete Guide to Asperger's Syndrome

ACKNOWLEDGEMENTS

A huge thanks to all the couples and individuals who have offered their feedback on many of the strategies described in this book. Without you this book would not have been possible. This book is written for you.

Thank you Professor Tony Attwood – you were the first to encourage me in my research and have over the years continued to offer support, encouragement and advice.

Thank you Jason Thompson for both support and the information given on alexithymia.

Thank you to Antony Corbett who gave his time and talent to drawing the sketches in this book.

Thank you to my son William who added the final touches to the artwork and drew the picture for the socialising handout.

Thank you to Shenny and Mark for sharing a piece of their lives to be included in this book.

A very special thank you to Peter for the encouragement, support and time he freely gave during the writing of this book. You helped me to make this book possible; no amount of words could express my appreciation.

A very big thank you to my beautiful children Zoe, Zara and William and my wonderful son-in-law Neil who is the proud father of my first grandchild, little Emily. Thank you for being a constant source of encouragement, support and motivation.

TERMINOLOGY

For ease of use I will refer to the person affected by Asperger syndrome as the 'AS partner' and the person not affected by Asperger syndrome – neurotypical – as the 'NT partner'.

I would also like to mention that this workbook is relevant to all couples, whether they be heterosexual, gay or lesbian. If one partner has Asperger syndrome then the problems that are presented in the relationship will be of a similar nature.

USING THIS BOOK

In this book you will find blank worksheets for you to fill in with your partner (or family member). You can either write on these worksheets directly or, if you prefer, you could copy them out.

INTRODUCTION

Making difference work

I have worked as a therapist with couples and families where one or more members are on the autistic spectrum for over ten years. In that time, I have developed strategies that have benefited both the person affected by Asperger syndrome (AS) and all their family members.

Living in a family where at least one member is affected by Asperger syndrome can have an impact on all the family members; all will be affected in some way, but not necessarily in the same way. Living with Asperger syndrome is quite different to living with any other disability. It is invisible, there are no apparent physical signs; in most cases it would appear that the AS family member is doing fine and coping. This appearance of being okay can cause expectations, particularly within communication and social interaction; expectations the AS partner may find difficulty in attaining.

Asperger syndrome will affect some of the fundamental ingredients required for relationships either to form or to be maintained. Sometimes relationships may struggle on for years in the belief that it will get better with time. Yet, in an intimate relationship, for example, neither of the couple is aware of what is causing the problems and persistent misunderstandings. This can wear down the mental and physical health of both and affect their self-esteem.

Asperger syndrome can affect a person's ability to empathise emotionally and communicate both verbally and non-verbally. It can affect the ability to express emotions and perceive the emotions of those around them. Most of my work as a therapist has focused on this aspect, in an endeavour to help my clients to find a different way to communicate so that they might understand and work together for the future of their relationship. It is often the obvious that needs addressing – the bringing together of two very different worlds – in order that both might understand and appreciate how these two worlds can be incorporated into a life together.

This book looks to provide a working basis for couples, either on their own or in conjunction with a therapist, to learn new strategies and ideas that will benefit their relationship together and as a family. Many of the ideas in this book come from years of research and years of counselling experience with hundreds of couples and families affected by Asperger syndrome. I do not advocate or propose a specific theory or model for working with couples and families as I believe that all individuals are different and each needs to be treated as a unique case. However, there are some fundamental areas that become problematic in an Asperger relationship.

Not all the strategies proffered here will apply in every situation. It will be through trial and error that a couple discover each other, discover what works for them and discover how their quality of life and self-esteem might be improved.

Chapter One

Understanding the Difference

The majority of couples that come to see me have been struggling to maintain their relationship and make things work for some time. Often they both feel exhausted, feel their resources are running out and that, despite their individual efforts, the same things keep going wrong, time and time again. Sometimes there is mention of how things used to be in the beginning, how when they first met it was a much happier time, not fraught with so many of the difficulties they now face. The neurotypical (NT) partner will often present as feeling drained and no longer having the energy to make things work. The AS partner may feel constantly under attack as though whatever they do it will never make the NT partner happy.

The different species concept

The NT partner and the AS partner are very different and could be described as different species, neither superior nor inferior, just different. In order to understand this let's think about the animal kingdom. In the animal kingdom there are lots of different species. Some are similar but the majority can be easily identified. Each individual species sticks together; they mate together and, for some, spend their lives together. They eat the same food and enjoy the same environment.

Although humans are a species in themselves there are derivatives, or sociological species, unconnected to variations in physical appearance, within that human species. We are biologically the same yet we are not necessarily psychologically, sociologically or emotionally the same.

Sometimes two people meet, think they have found a partner who is in tune with them, feel happier than they have for some time and enjoy the new partner's company intensely. Later, this seems to wane for them as differences that were somewhat overlooked in the initial euphoria begin to surface.

Let's imagine an Eagle (male) meets a Zebra (female). Both are entranced by the uniqueness of each other and they fall in love. They are really happy until one day Eagle flys off into the sky with a view to finding Zebra something really nice to eat. Eagle hunts all day until a hare is caught and, with much effort, flies back with his catch all the way to Zebra's front door.

'Surprise! Surprise!' says Eagle, really excited. 'Look what I have caught for you to eat!'

Zebra is shocked as the dead hare is espied and says, 'But I do not eat meat!' Eagle is mortified and feels rejected; all that effort given little or no recognition; the risk to life and limb to bring such a gift now spurned. At this point the whole relationship changes as Eagle and Zebra recognise that, although they might share the same environment, might enjoy mutual aspects of that environment, they do not share a need for the same food. Zebra is a herd animal and finds it lonely in Eagle's remote world. Eagle loves Zebra and wants the best for Zebra. Eagle provides everything except that which Zebra really wants or needs – food. Zebra will compromise and try to fit into Eagle's world.

Zebra needs Eagle to be close, attentive and loving, while Eagle needs to rationalise, calculate and be a provider. Zebra thrives on vegetation. Eagle is a meat eater and does not understand why Zebra rejects that which Eagle worked so hard to provide. The result is that Zebra slowly begins to deteriorate from lack of the food she needs to survive and the herding instinct of her own species. This leaves Eagle feeling very hurt. Whatever he does, it does not seem to make Zebra happy and he feels unappreciated for all his efforts.

Different needs

Although human beings are a single species, within that species exist variations that are not as obviously different physically as Eagle and Zebra, but nonetheless exhibiting the selfsame emotional and logical disparity. The NT partner and the AS partner think in very different ways. Both need a very different type of food and for many a very different environment too. The AS partners need their food to be logical and practical as their thought processing is quite linear and focused, lending them to being structured rather than empathic. Most AS partners enjoy being a couple but what they require from their partner emotionally is often minimal and when they fail to make their NT partner happy they can become quite distressed.

The NT partner's needs are quite different. They require their food to be emotional, even idiosyncratic, as their thought processing may be romantic and idealistic, lending them to be adaptable rather than fixed. Most NT partners thrive upon the emotional reflection their partner gives them. However, the absence of this reflection will leave them feeling deprived. Unaware that their partner is being deprived of something they are unable to offer, the AS partner experiences a sense of unhappiness as their partner appears not to be as content as they are within the relationship. Neither knows how to change this. They may decide it must be something they are doing wrong or sometimes, even worse, they decide it is the other's fault and attempt to make them feel guilty.

Becoming aware of or recognising their differences, particularly where Asperger syndrome exists within a relationship, can be a watershed for change. Up until this point the NT partner and the AS partner were probably unaware of their differences, unaware of their different needs, and sought – potentially detrimentally – to compromise. The NT partner, being more empathic, will have recognised that the AS partner often prefers to be in a solitary environment. The NT partner will come to know that the AS partner cannot feed her, know that she cannot live off the AS partner's food alone, but will stand by the AS partner, believing there is a future together, believing that things can change.

It is likely to be the NT partner who will spend most of the time trying to live in the AS partner's environment, as the AS partner does not have the necessary skills to live in the NT partner's world. The longer the NT partner is outside of their environment, deprived of the food they need, the more likely the NT partner will start to lose their identity and become more like the AS partner. The NT partner needs to take care and not let this happen, trying to ensure their needs are met.

As long as neither depends on the other for their food and as long as they make time to be in their respective environments, it is totally possible for the NT partner and the AS partner to enjoy a life together. If both have enough love, commitment and respect for each other within the relationship, then all things are possible. This workbook provides some strategies to help make that possible. There will always be difficulties and struggles when living with another equal but different species, which this book won't change. However, with understanding and acceptance of those differences, allied with a determination by both people to have that life together, improvements in their situation will follow.

A different way of thought processing

In order to be able to understand and accept the differences that exist, a couple will need to understand what it is that makes them think differently, express themselves differently and, in some cases, appear to love each other differently. To explain this I use the example of research carried out by Rita Carter, author of the excellent book *Mapping the Mind* (1998). I have already written about this research in my book *Aspergers in Love* (Aston 2003b). Since then I have adapted this explanation in a way that makes sense to my clients and helps to understand both themselves and their partner.

Carter used positron emission tomography (PET), a brain scanning technique that produces a three-dimensional, visual image of the functional processes of the brain. A PET scan can make it possible to see what is happening in the brain and show the areas that are in use at a particular time and with a specific context. Carter used PET scans on people who had been diagnosed with Asperger syndrome and people who were not affected by Asperger syndrome. What she discovered was particularly enlightening, giving an insight into the differences in thought processing between the NT partner and the AS partner. First, Carter asked each group in the study a logical problem-solving question. Each group was able to come up with the answer by using logic and for each group an area in the left hemisphere of the frontal lobes lit up on the scan.

Second, she asked each group a question that required theory of mind to answer the question correctly. Theory of mind is the ability to appreciate the perception of another, the part of the brain that governs empathy and insight. Carter found that in the NT participants another part of the brain lit up on the scan. This area was just below the area of the brain that governed logic. The NT participants were quick to answer the question correctly. However, in the AS participants this part of their brain did not show any activity. Instead the logical part of the brain became active. This suggests that the AS participants were attempting to work out another's behaviour using logic, but people are not necessarily logical when it comes to behaviour. It is therefore likely that the AS participant's answer could be wrong (unless they had experienced a similar situation and were able to recall an appropriate answer). It will usually take them longer to find an answer as it will be through logic rather than empathy that they find it.

This does not suggest that the AS participant has no theory of mind, but it may suggest that theory of mind has not fully developed. A typical developing four-year-old child would be able to pass tests on the ability to apply theory of mind, whereas with children affected by Asperger syndrome theory of mind does not begin to develop until the child is between 9 and 14 years old (Happe and Frith 1995). This implies that in children affected by Asperger syndrome awareness that other people have different mind states, separate from their own, may never develop beyond the very basic level. It is unlikely that development will ever progress to the second stage of understanding – that of appreciating that other people actually have their own thoughts and feelings, or of having the ability to reflect and consider that others have these separate thoughts and feelings all of their own (Happe and Frith 1995).

Lack of theory of mind has been proposed as the core deficit in the AS partner and its impact has been found at all developmental levels throughout the life span (Ozonoff, Roger and Pennington 1991). The development of theory of mind is essential in order to empathise with another; to see and understand the perspective of another; to relate to another's state of mind; to understand that another's mind state is separate from one's own. This does not mean the AS partner cannot care or show sympathy (sympathy and empathy are two quite different things) as the majority of the AS partners I encounter do care about their partner and family. However, they will not be able to perceive what it is like for either their partner or family. It is this difference that will have the greatest impact on a couple's relationship as it will be responsible for the majority of misunderstandings, consequently leading to both struggling to understand what it is that keeps breaking down between them.

Another important aspect of these differences will be the impact upon the partners individually, particularly on the AS partner, as they will be trying to work out everything by applying logic. For example, when the AS partner enters a room full of people or joins a group situation, they will not only be trying to work out the environment with logic, but they will also try and use logic to work out the people they encounter. The AS partner's brain will have to work very hard to keep up to speed with conversation in a group situation. In a more intimate or emotional situation the AS partner will struggle with many of the nuances of communication, as will often occur when the AS partner is with the NT partner.

The AS partner's brain will be trying to apply logic to the facial expressions, body language and intonation of people, often falling behind as trying to think of suitable responses will cause delay. Distractions such as peripheral movement or background noises will also impinge upon the AS partner. The list goes on

– it is no wonder that the AS partner can go into overload or meltdown. There is basically too much information for the logical brain to process and adequately respond to. If the AS partner or others involved in the situation do not recognise this potential meltdown in time, and make an effort to call a halt to what is happening, then the AS partner's brain will reach a point of total overload. The brain will then assume it is under threat and in defence will send the AS partner into either flight or fight. Fight will be an aggressive reaction, maybe verbal abuse, while flight may mean an abrupt walking out. The brain has shut down. The AS partner is no longer able to participate in the situation and will retreat and walk away until control over their thoughts is regained and processing returns to normal.

It is very likely that after the event the AS partner's recollection of what happened may be different to what actually happened, potentially sparking off another heated discussion between the AS partner and the NT partner. The NT partner may believe the AS partner is not being honest or is trying to change the truth. This is not necessarily the case as, due to the overload in the AS partner's brain, information will have been lost. This will not be because of the AS partner's failure to remember, but because the data never reached the AS partner's long-term memory. The overload and extreme stress of the situation can cause information to be lost. Both the AS partner and the NT partner may have a very different perspective of what happened. This can be confusing and frustrating for both of them. It can have a detrimental effect upon the trust between them, especially if either believe the other is being dishonest or manipulating the truth.

A different perspective

To understand how a couple can be in the same place at the same time and yet have such different perspectives, imagine two people standing back to back on the top of a mountain. One is the NT partner and the other the AS partner. The AS partner's view is of a city and consists of buildings, trains, cars and factories. The NT partner's view is of the countryside and they can see a river, wildlife and a colourful meadow. Both are stood in the same place at the same time and yet both are seeing very different views, so their respective perceptions of the same place are radically different. Later when they discuss it both are surprised and taken aback by the different memory they both have of the experience and will struggle to figure out why their respective perspectives are so different.

This is how different perspectives can occur. Neither is lying or being manipulative but simply seeing things from a different point of view. However, just because they are aware that they see things differently or accept they process information differently, this does not mean it will be any easier for the couple to deal with the misunderstandings. It is useful to understand why the difference exists – understanding can make such a difference to the relationship and the self-esteem of both. In therapy I find the first and most relevant area that needs to be addressed is their different communication methods and how each needs to learn a way of understanding the other's language.

Chapter
Two
COMMUNICATION

Communication is the area often highlighted as the cause of most of the problems in the relationship. The couple may report a history of misunderstandings, feeling unheard, feeling criticised and not getting the point. Over a period of time this may have resulted in the AS partner refusing to communicate at all, especially if they feel the subject matter is going to lead to a confrontation. For the AS partner there is likely to be a history of unintentionally getting it wrong and they may have learnt that it is far better not to say anything at all. For the NT partner, this reluctance to communicate or express feelings will be read as rejection and a lack of caring, increasing the NT partner's frustration. The AS partner may believe that the NT partner is really angry, leading to the AS partner withdrawing further, and so the cycle goes on.

It will take time, patience and commitment by the couple to change their communication methods. It will be hard work as a pattern will have evolved between the couple that will make it quite difficult for them to spot the triggers which cause the communication failures. Finding an appropriate therapist to work on communication with them can feel less critical for the couple, as the therapist can act as an unbiased third party, observe the interactions between the couple and reflect back to them where improvements could be made. It is often easier to hear this from someone impartial whom the couple are comfortable with and whose observations won't be taken personally.

However, if it has not been possible to find a therapist to work with, a couple can still use the worksheets in this book and experiment together until a way can be found that works for both of them.

Communicating on different wavelengths

The first step in improving communication is to understand why it breaks down in the first place. Imagine two transceivers, both able to receive and transmit information, where, unbeknown to either, their wavelengths are different. One is tuned for logical FM while the other is tuned for emotional FM. Logical FM suits the AS partner as it works in a linear way, transmitting one message at a time and receiving from one transmitter at a time. Emotional FM suits the NT partner as it works in an unpredictable way, transmitting multiple messages and receiving from multiple transmitters. Both are using the same waveband (FM), but neither is capable of the tuning required to interpret messages from the other transmitter.

Logic transmission versus emotional transmission

Imagine two transceivers – the first one can only transmit and receive on a logical wavelength, the transmissions will be linear, one subject at a time and have a beginning and an end.

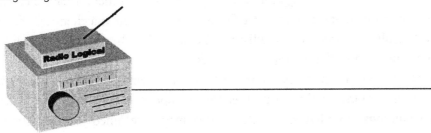

The second transceiver transmits in a very different way – it uses an emotional wavelength. This is quite different to the former and consists of up and downs, zigzags and loops. It can transmit many messages at the same time and does not have a precise beginning or end.

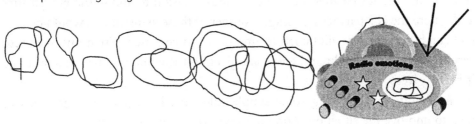

When these two transmitters try to communicate the result is going to be a complete breakdown in communication, leaving both feeling unheard and misunderstood.

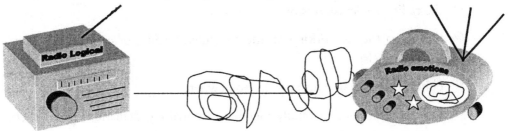

One thing at a time

The example of the two transceivers illustrates well an important aspect in the difference between the AS partner and the NT partner. Clients I see are often already aware that the AS partner struggles with multitasking and can be distracted easily by noises or things that are happening around them. I have a clock in my therapy room that often finds itself outside in reception as a client will have found it difficult to concentrate on what was being said as they found themselves constantly tuning in to the ticking of the clock.

The NT partner needs to be aware of this when communicating with their partner as distractions for the AS partner can disrupt communication and make misunderstandings more likely. The AS partner may have tuned in to a distraction and not be receiving the message which the NT partner is sending. Messages given in this state are in danger of being lost or misunderstood by the AS partner. When the purpose of the message is raised later and the AS partner appears to have completely forgotten what was said, it can lead to disagreements. The NT partner could, first, believe that the AS partner was not bothered about what was said and had dismissed it as irrelevant because it was said by the NT partner or, second, that the AS partner made a conscious decision to annoy the NT partner and ignore the NT partner's message. Neither of these assumptions would be correct and both partners will be left feeling hurt and confused. Situations like these can be avoided if thought and effort are given to the context in which a message is being given.

Applying and following some simple rules that both partners agree to can help to improve the situation. Add your own to the end of the list.

Rules for giving important messages

Important messages should never be given when:

- the radio or television is on
- the AS partner is working on the computer, reading or concentrating on something else
- either partner is in a hurry to go somewhere
- the children or other family members are making demands upon either partner

- either partner is feeling stressed

- the AS partner has just arrived home from work

- the family or partners are eating

- either partner is driving the car

- in a group situation such as a dinner party or while out with friends.

It is important always to use the AS partner's name at the beginning of the message. This really useful strategy was offered by Wendy Lawson at a conference I attended. Wendy Lawson, who has Asperger syndrome and wrote the informative book *Sex, Sexuality and the Autistic Spectrum* (2005), recommended that having used the person's name to open the message, they should count to ten and then repeat the person's name followed by the message. Lawson explained that this time was needed for the person with Asperger syndrome to make the transition in their brain from what they were doing to receiving the message. Lawson did suggest that counting to ten was dependent on the person receiving the message and could be adapted if a longer or shorter count was needed.

Memory aids

Another successful strategy that can be applied to ensure messages are received and remembered is the use of physical reminders which the AS partner either can refer to, or is automatically prompted to. This not only makes important messages more concrete but also gives the AS partner a tool to aid memory. Reminders that can be used are:

- post-it notes
- written lists
- mobile phone alerts
- letters
- emails
- whiteboards
- noticeboards.

As I said earlier, there is no guarantee that a given method will work for a given couple, so I always advise a couple to experiment and find out what works best for them. It will be by trial and error that a couple will work out what is best.

The more stressed the AS partner becomes, the more they will struggle with memory and communication. This can make the AS partner appear more affected by Asperger syndrome. Keeping stress to a minimum is beneficial to all concerned. One cause of stress for the AS partner can be when they are expected or are being pressured to express their feelings or to work out someone else's feelings. There are ways to alleviate this and make life easier for both partners and other family members.

Expressing feelings

One reason for communication breakdown can be the inability of the AS partner either to express their own feelings or appreciate their partner's feelings. This is called alexithymia, a Greek term meaning (literally) without words for feelings. Alexithymia is the inability to express emotions or understand others' emotions. It affects 85 per cent of those affected by an autistic spectrum disorder (Hill, Berthoz and Frith 2004). As well as exhibiting alexithymia, someone affected by Asperger syndrome, whose theory of mind will be underdeveloped (Beaumont and Newcombe 2006), will have an inability to fully empathise, finding it difficult to understand someone else's thoughts, feelings or perspectives (Thompson 2008).

This lack of empathy can cause problems and often a complete breakdown in communication, which will be upsetting and disturbing for both in the relationship. Being put under pressure to express feelings can be almost painful for the AS partner and the more pressure that is exerted, the more they are likely to withdraw and say nothing at all. This can make the NT partner feel totally unloved and rejected or left thinking, 'My AS partner cannot love me because if they did they would be able to tell me how they feel.'

Some individuals with Asperger syndrome will simply reply, when asked how they feel, that they are okay or fine, not even attempting to say that in fact they are quite sad, frustrated or anxious. This is counterproductive as the AS partner can be left feeling unacknowledged and still trying to cope with the issues that are bothering them, while the NT partner may either just presume that everything is okay or, more likely, that everything is not okay and presume their partner is not confiding in them or is hiding something. The result of this will be that the NT partner might keep asking what is wrong, resulting in further withdrawal by the AS partner.

Feelings in colour

The idea of replacing feelings with colours has been around for some time. I developed a way of making this work for couples and families affected by Asperger syndrome. It is a technique I teach to my clients and in my workshops. Its success is high as its simplicity makes it of use in all situations, for all family members. Just the couple can use it or the whole family can be involved. I have found it works just as well with children as it does with adults. It can be developed with a therapist or it can be put together in the privacy of your home. Whichever is chosen, it should be fun putting it together and putting it to use.

When I put a colour chart together for a couple, it is important that they choose the expressions and colours which work for them as the chart must have meaning for them when they are using it. They will both be able to apply it to each other to discover what is happening for each. As an example, I often suggest two colours for anger such as red and orange, where red can mean 'angry with you' and orange can mean 'angry with something else'. Many AS partners have discussed the difficulty they have in figuring out why their partner appears angry. They often assume it is because of something they have done. This will cause them stress and may lead them to withdraw at a time when their partner may need them to talk or offer a hug. If the AS partner is able to ask the colour their NT partner feels, the reply, if orange for example, will tell the AS partner that their partner's anger is about something else and not anything they have done.

Another category I encourage is a colour for needing space – this is often white. For the AS family member stressful situations can build up, especially at work or school where there can be a collection of stressful moments throughout the day. The AS individual will be working hard to keep pace with communication, working out what to say and how to say it, all things which can lead to meltdown. Having space or a quiet time simply to catch up and process what has gone on can be vital to their well being. Thirty minutes or an hour out to listen to music or to participate in their special interest will allow them this space. In the longer term all will benefit as the AS individual will find it far easier to communicate and interact. Having this time to destress and process will be of real benefit to the AS individual. Often though, the AS partner will feel guilty about saying 'I want to be alone' or 'Please will you not talk to me for an hour', especially when just home from work, having not seen their NT partner all day. Being able to say 'I feel white' should reduce any feelings of rejection as their partner then knows this is not about them and in a short time things should be back to normal.

The Feelings in Colour chart is a very useful tool for couples and families. Coloured postcards are available from many craft shops, which could be bought, cut to an appropriate size and used by partners or family. It is a great way of working with children and adolescents who become upset or frustrated about things at school but are unable to express those feelings to their parents.

Adding numbers

An essential addition to using colours as a method to describe feelings is to add a value to those colours. It is not always enough to know that a person is red (angry) or black (depressed) as they could be slightly angry or very depressed. To ask the AS partner how angry or depressed they are may lead to further anger or depression as they may not be able to describe this in words. This question can cause frustration and the wrong reaction, leaving the NT partner feeling hurt that their attempt at showing care or concern for their partner's feelings has been rejected, making things worse.

The use of numbers can alleviate this. Once again it is simple to use and easy to apply; it works in any given situation whether private or public. Words to describe feelings can be abstract or perceptual in meaning. Words are often not definitive enough for AS partners. It is easier for them to make sense of feelings if they can do so by applying logic and making them finite.

This is how colours and numbers work together. If I ask a client with Asperger syndrome to imagine what colour anger would be, the answer is often red. I ask if they can picture this colour in their mind, or I will give them a red card to look at. Using a number chart from one to ten I will say, 'Okay, if ten is the deepest red and one is the faintest red, how red are you today?' Their answer will tell me immediately how angry they feel as numbers are often tangible for them.

The example shows a chart that I filled in with a young man I was working with. For him black meant suicidal thoughts. Upon entering the counselling room, although he outwardly appeared to be okay, I asked him what colour he was, to which he replied black. I asked him how black and he answered eleven and a half! In that reply I knew that this was urgent and in need of immediate attention. I could have wasted a whole hour trying to encourage my client to tell me what was going on for him to no avail. I call this method a cognitive shortcut.

The Feelings in Colour chart of

Peter

Angry at you .... | Red

Angry at someone else .... | Orange

Sad/Down/Suicidal .... | Black

Happy .... | Yellow

Confused .... | Green

Needing space .... | White

Feeling criticised .... | Purple

Need a hug .... | Pink

Feeling rejected .... | Grey

0   1   2   3   4   5   6   7   8   9   10

For couples and families a colour for love is a useful addition. The importance of expressing love can often be overlooked in a couple's busy life. Sometimes the AS partner will just assume their partner knows they are loved, if only because of the things they do for them or because they told them a year ago or when they first met. Being told they are loved is food for the NT partner. The more this is expressed, the happier and more secure the NT partner will feel. With the couples I work with, this is a topic that comes up very often. I may ask the AS partner, 'Do you love your partner?' to which they invariably answer, 'Yes'. I then ask, 'Do you tell your partner you love them?' to which they usually answer, 'They already know I do.' By enquiring further it is usually the case that the AS partner finds the words difficult or the words they do find feel false. Additionally, having said the words, when pressed with 'How much?' the reply might be 'I do not know' or 'I am not sure' – not very flattering or reassuring for the NT partner. The AS partner who is able to say 'I am feeling pink' (love) and when asked, 'How much?' can say 'six' or 'nine' will be on surer ground, thus leaving the NT partner reassured that they are loved.

Using more than one colour at a time is similar to feeling more than one emotion at a time. Someone might be feeling criticised and sad, or they may feel happy and excited. I have worked with clients who went into great detail, using their colours and numbers, to express how they felt. For example, asking what colour my client is today may elicit the following: 'I am a two for brown (anxious), green (confused) is seven and yellow is one (happy).' Some clients will use percentages while others will enjoy using descriptions such as 'black with green streaks', or 'yellow with a grey outline'.

This method is versatile and adaptive and can be tailored to suit the person using it. It will not work for everyone, but for those it does work for it makes problems with emotional expression a thing of the past.

Instructions for using the Feelings in Colour chart

1   Have a selection of coloured crayons using as many colours as possible.

2   Think about an emotion most likely to come up for you, e.g. anger.

3   Enter the emotion on the line before the box.

4   Choose a colour that is representative of this emotion. If you are using the Feelings in Colour chart as a family, then choose the colours between you.

5   Use this colour to fill in the box that links to the emotion.

6   Repeat steps 2–4 until as many boxes as required are filled in. If more are needed use a new sheet.

7   Make copies of these so all relevant people can make use of them.

8   Use the colour chart and numbers together to gain a deeper and quicker insight into how the person is feeling.

The Feelings in Colour chart of

....

....

....

....

....

....

....

....

....

0 1 2 3 4 5 6 7 8 9 10

The card communication system

Making the relationship between an AS partner and an NT partner work will mean the couple experimenting until they find ways to communicate – ways that they can both understand and translate correctly – otherwise communication will continue to fail. This means that both have to become more aware of each other's differences and try to accept them.

The AS partner can be very sensitive to perceived criticism and has probably had a lifetime's experience of having 'got it wrong' going right back to their childhood. The AS partner will be inclined to hear criticism where none was intended. The AS partner needs to be aware of their sensitivity and make a real effort to check with their NT partner when they perceive criticism. The AS partner needs to be able to ask the NT partner to be more specific about what they are saying. The AS partner needs to try and resist the instinct to shut down or become defensive before the NT partner has had the chance to explain what they are trying to say.

The NT partner, on the other hand, will be trying to learn a new way of communicating, learning to use logic rather than emotion with their partner. There is no easy step but one way of doing this is to change the medium by which the message is conveyed, using visual forms of communication rather than words.

Let me explain. A difficult and sensitive issue has been raised which, due to poor reception and translation, has been lost. Both partners are feeling frustrated at not being understood and if it continues someone may lose their temper or say something they will regret. The NT partner, in their frustration, may turn and say, 'I've had enough of this! I am tired of trying to explain something so simple that you make such hard work of for me. I can only think it is because you do not care enough to try and understand!'

The NT partner would like the AS partner to respond, 'Of course I care, I am trying to understand. Let's just have a hug for now and come back to this later.' Unfortunately, it is more likely that the AS partner will have heard this as direct criticism, interpreting it as 'My partner thinks I am stupid and a failure as a partner.' This is all part of the transmitter not being able to receive and translate the message correctly, especially since by now the AS partner is teetering on the edge of a meltdown.

The AS partner is likely to walk away with a brain that feels like it is going to explode from emotional overload, having reached a point of either being unable to find the words or fearing that whatever they say at this point will be the wrong thing. This will reinforce the NT partner's view that the AS partner does not care enough to resolve the issue and does not even want to try. The NT partner may shout after the AS partner that if the AS partner walks away one more time the relationship is over, thus reinforcing the AS partner's perception that the NT partner cannot stand them and wants out of the relationship.

The relationship may become insecure and distrustful and the self-esteem of both may be plummeting. The original issue will not be raised or resolved, as both will feel too fragile to return to it for fear of repeating the same communication breakdown. This is an example of an absolute breakdown between the couple. This could have been avoided by using what I call a carding system. If we take the scenario at the point where the AS partner was becoming confused or unsure of what the NT partner was saying, they could have said, 'This is a yellow card situation.' This would signal to the NT partner to pause and track back to a point where the AS partner is able to say, 'This is a green card situation', green card meaning they understand what the discussion is about, allowing them to then continue the discussion. This use of yellow and green cards will, it is hoped, help the couple to avoid that absolute breakdown.

However, if the situation does reach the point where frustrations are about to be expressed negatively, then that partner should be able to say, 'This is a red card situation', rather than the potentially hurtful or destructive words they might use. Whereupon the discussion ends but the door is left open for it to resume at a later date without recriminations on either side.

Words are easy to misinterpret, especially in the heat of an argument. This system uses cards instead of words, and these cards can be shown or spoken. The use of the green card can be useful as it tells the other partner 'I'm okay, I understand', while the yellow card says 'I'm not sure. Can you try and explain differently?' If the situation manages to go beyond these, then the red card allows for that pause without the situation degenerating further.

Example of the card communication system

Red card stands for Danger.

We need to stop this debate right now.

We cannot sort this out at the moment.

I am frightened this will get out of control.

I am too upset to continue.

I do not want to say anything that will hurt you.

Yellow card stands for Uncertainty.

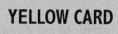

I do not fully understand what you mean.

Please tell me in a way that I can understand.

Can you go back and explain again, please?

I am unsure as to what you want me to do.

Green card means I am okay.

I understand what you are saying.

I feel okay with what you have told me.

Instructions for using the card system

1   Decide exactly what you both want each card to mean.

2   Agree together situations that you might apply the card system to.

3   Decide whether you would rather use an actual card or just say, 'This is a … card situation!'

4   If the red card is called, then both must respect this and allow the other time out.

5   An arrangement to readdress the situation will need to be made so it is not just ignored, as unresolved issues do not go away.

Card communication system

Red card stands for Danger.

Put your own card meanings:

Yellow card stands for Uncertainty.

Put your own card meanings:

Green card means I am okay.

Put your own card meanings:

It is important the card system is not used as a way of totally avoiding particular topics or issues. The red card does not mean the subject is closed. It needs to be understood by both that they will return to the subject at a later date which suits both. Ignored issues are unresolved issues, and unresolved issues come back to haunt so they will need to be addressed at some point. If the couple are in therapy, then they can take the unresolved issue to the therapy where, in an environment safe for both, the therapist may be able to offer different perspectives or strategies for the couple.

The card communication system can be used at different times for different reasons. It is a way of letting the other person know clearly how each feels without the use of words, which may be interpreted as hurtful or rejecting. The system can be used to let the other partner know or reassure the other partner that sense is being made of what's being said and that things are okay. When something feels ambiguous or one partner feels they are missing the point, then the system can also help. With practice the card communication system will soon become a habit and leave room for less ambiguity and misunderstanding.

Sometimes the carding system will not be appropriate and an argument will occur, which in itself can be a healthy process if certain rules are followed. The couple need to remind themselves of the different wavelengths they operate upon and consider the following.

Three rules for good arguing

I suggest couples follow three very important rules for good arguing. If these are followed, arguing can become a healthy debate in which both can share their different perspectives without the fear of confrontation.

First rule: No physical abuse

Second rule: No verbal abuse

Third rule: No bringing up the past

First rule: No physical abuse

Physical abuse should not be tolerated in any relationship. Just because a couple are an NT and AS combination does not make this maxim less so. Physical abuse breaks all the rules that govern respect for the safety and well being of the other person during a discussion or argument. It rips apart the very core of the relationship and leaves it feeling controlled, under threat and intimidating.

In my research (Aston 2003a) I found that the majority of AS partners would rather stay in a dysfunctional relationship in which they were being abused than leave and live alone, partly due to fear of change and partly due to the dependency that can develop on the NT partner. On the other hand, the NT partner may stay in the relationship in which they are being abused because they live in hope that their partner will change.

Second rule: No verbal abuse

Verbal abuse is a form of control by one person towards another. The verbally abused person is stripped of their self-worth, self-esteem and confidence in their abilities. Verbal abuse can be painful, destructive and have long-term psychological effects. Using sarcasm, double meanings or humour at the expense of another are forms of verbal abuse and should be avoided at all times. Shouting, stamping of feet or slamming of doors are forms of verbal abuse, as these are audible expressions designed to intimidate and control.

Third rule: No bringing up the past

Bringing up the past is often used to make the other partner feel guilty. This is unfair as neither partner can change what has already happened. The best either partner can ever do is learn from their experiences and try to do things differently in the future.

Unfortunately, due to the frequent breakdown of communication between AS and NT partners, there may be many unresolved issues. This may be due to a belief that the other partner will not understand or get the point, or either partner fears that the raising of issues will make things worse. Consequently, issues get stored up. I call this 'pebbles in the bucket' as with each unresolved issue each partner adds a pebble to their bucket. When an argument ensues, they turn to their respective buckets and proceed to throw the pebbles at one another.

Strategies to avoid breaking the rules

The difficulty is in realising that a point has been reached where a breach of the rules is about to occur. For example, a couple may be discussing an issue where one partner is doing most of the talking and dominating the discussion. The other partner is sat quietly, saying little, even with a benign expression, and there are no outward indications that they are becoming either frustrated or angry. How does either know they need to pause before this explodes into violence or verbal abuse?

One way is the Feelings in Colour chart that I have already explained (p.29–35), where the AS partner can have an accurate method of expression by using the numbers to express the extent of frustration or anger. However, if this does not work and relating to colours proves difficult, then it may help to visualise an active object and relate it to the build-up of feeling the AS person is experiencing. For some this can be a pressure cooker. In this instance I have used the frustration or anger thermometer, as suggested by Tony Attwood in his book *Asperger's Syndrome: A Guide for Parents and Professionals* (1998). The anger thermometer, as its name suggests, is more applicable to situations that are building up to danger point.

The frustration or anger thermometer

I ask clients to visualise a thermometer, or better still I show them a picture of a thermometer. I ask them to try and picture the red liquid rising as the temperature rises, suggesting they think of their frustration or anger as a rising temperature on a scale of one to ten. How high does their thermometer have to go before control is lost? Six? Seven? By keeping this number in mind the AS partner can convey to their partner that their level of frustration or anger is reaching danger point, whereupon preventative measures can be implemented to calm the situation.

Taking the example of the couple who are having the one-sided discussion, the partner who is doing most of the talking could stop and ask their partner what number their thermometer has reached. Conversely, the partner feeling frustrated or angry could simply interject with 'My thermometer is at seven', thus informing the other that it's time to pause.

This use of the thermometer works for both NT and AS partners, so long as they have agreed that as soon as the other partner indicates their boiling point is approaching, they break off and apply a calming strategy. These calming strategies will be different for different people. For example, many of the adolescents I work with find music very therapeutic. Music can be mood altering and some AS people are highly tuned in to rhythmic sound. If seven is the recognised level that can be reached on the thermometer whilst still maintaining control, then when that point is reached allowing the AS person to step back and plug into their iPod or MP3 player, for example, will potentially alleviate the frustration or anger, avoiding breaking the good arguing rules.

For others the calming strategy might be to use deep breathing techniques, to find a quiet place to sit, or to become absorbed in a special interest. Once again it is trial and error in finding what works for each individual. Both partners can make use of this technique. Couples and families need to find out what works for the AS person in order to allow them to apply the calming strategies that work without the AS person feeling guilty or prevented from using that strategy.

Although I talk about the AS partner here, these techniques work equally well for the NT partner when faced with the possibility of an eruption into abusive behaviour.

The thermometer can be applied whenever any of the three rules is in danger of being broken and where this slow build-up appears to be happening. However, not every situation has a slow build-up. Sometimes a reaction can appear out of the blue; a strong reaction which a partner wasn't expecting; a reaction which could lead them to react strongly as well. It may have been how something was said, or perceived to have been said. I mentioned sarcasm and double meanings earlier. Many AS partners have had a lifetime, usually starting with bullying at school, of this type of abuse and can often misinterpret something the NT partner has said.

A partner may overreact in a subliminal attempt to start an argument; an argument that will allow unresolved issues to be discussed. Many NT partners find it difficult to get their AS partner to talk. This subconscious reaction is often due to the weight of their 'bucket of pebbles'. Arguments and discussions are healthy so long as the three rules are not broken. It is difficult, considering the two previous paragraphs, to take a deep breath, think of the three rules and not break them.

Having received an overreaction, the partner needs to pause and consider using the whole sentence strategy (Aston 2001).

Whole sentence strategy

When an argument ensues, a tirade of statements, accusations and innuendo flows forth, leading to further aggravation of the situation. Having had an unexpected overreaction from their partner, either partner should try and apply whole, single sentences to the situation; for example, 'I can see what I have just said has upset you. That was not my intention. Can you explain to me what it is that upset you?' Further application of this whole sentence strategy can be seen in the following examples.

Example 1: Avoiding the 'you' word

On the way home after an evening out at a very expensive restaurant, where the NT partner became unhappy with their AS partner's attitude to others, he or she says, 'Did you have to be so rude to everyone? I cannot believe how you spoke to that waitress. You ruined the whole evening by your stupid childish tantrum!'

The use of 'you' in an argumentative tone is often heard as direct criticism and can be antagonistic. Using whole sentences without the use of 'you' can keep the situation calmer. Our NT partner could have said, 'I realise how annoying the waitress was after having waited so long for our meal. However, I felt very embarrassed by some of the things that were said. Can we discuss how to find a better way of dealing with this in the future?'

Example 2: Picking an appropriate moment

The AS partner has just walked in from work. The television is on, the children are playing up and the dog wants to go out. The NT partner is annoyed and says, 'How could you forget you were meeting me at the school? You do not give a damn about getting this statement for Thomas. All you care about is your work. I may as well be a single parent. At least I would get the extra support.'

It is likely the AS partner had completely forgotten the appointment and is totally bemused at the situation they have arrived home to and there's a good chance they will withdraw by escaping with the dog. A more appropriate time to discuss this may have been later in the evening, after the children have gone to bed. The NT partner could say, 'I was expecting us to meet at the school today to discuss Thomas's statement. I felt very alone without you. I wonder if it's worth starting to use a diary/computer/palm reader?'

Example 3: Being sensitive to the situation

The AS partner has just come home from work. The NT partner is busy cooking dinner in the kitchen. Having noticed the hall is a bit messy, the AS partner says, 'I see the hall floor needs vacuuming.' Not a very flattering hello and from it the NT partner will have probably heard, 'What have you been doing all day?'

Arriving home is an important time. Neither partner knows what sort of day the other has had. Therefore an initial friendly or loving greeting does help. It would be better if our AS partner did not mention the hall floor at all. However, once something has been noticed, our AS partner will find it very hard not to mention it. So a kinder way might have been, 'Hello dear/sweetheart (kiss). Shall I give the hall floor a quick vac round before we eat?'

Example 4: Saying what you mean

A couple is going out for the evening. The NT partner has just finished getting ready when the AS partner enters the bedroom and says, 'Are you going to get ready then? We're due there at seven thirty.'

This is not a good start to the evening. It is likely that the AS partner either had something in mind for the NT partner to wear or simply hadn't noticed they had changed. If the AS partner does have something in mind, then perhaps they could say, 'You're looking lovely. I was hoping you would wear (particular item) tonight. I really like you in that.'

These four examples, two for each partner to consider, highlight how the NT partner, being more emotionally adept, is prone to overelaborate but is able to pause and reword what they want to say, while the AS partner, being more logically adept, does not say enough but can learn that certain situations need certain responses.

Unresolved issues

I mentioned earlier the 'pebbles in a bucket' each partner may be carrying around, ready to throw at each other when a disagreement occurs. The best way of preventing a store of unresolved issues from accumulating, or a collection of negative distorted memories from developing, is to resolve the issues when they happen or shortly afterwards. The use of the colour chart, thermometer or applying whole sentences to avoid misunderstandings may work. Sometimes these may be inappropriate. An issue may come to light while one partner is alone. Having had a chance to brood upon it, they may not tackle the situation well when the couple are next together. It may be that a series of issues is coming to a head and needs dealing with.

Dealing with unresolved issues is best timed for when the couple are not angry or at loggerheads with each other. This can feel difficult for both as when they are getting on well it can seem destructive to risk bringing up an issue that may destroy the harmony. This is why unresolved issues are often only raised when the couple have already fallen out, so taking the risk of bringing up even more issues is of no consequence.

Keeping to the analogy of pebbles in the bucket, I have worked with couples to make this analogy real. I recommend they each buy a bucket, not too big, maybe a child's sandcastle bucket. When an issue comes up that bothers them and is unresolved, they should write it down briefly on a post-it note or piece of paper and put it in their bucket.

When the timing feels right and the couple have time and are not stressed, they should take just one unresolved issue out of each bucket and discuss it together or bring it to discuss with a therapist.

Unresolved issues can be easier to write down than to say. The written word is easier for the AS partner to deliberate upon and process. Having a sheet made for this purpose is useful. The following is an example of how it could be laid out. Always remember to stick to only one issue at a time. If it feels as if there are many issues, then these must be sorted with the most pressing at the top. If an issue has become too sensitive to bring up or work out together, it may be an idea to take that issue to therapy where it can be approached in the safety of the therapy room.

Instructions for using the Unresolved Issues sheets

1   Decide what is the most important issue for you to be resolved.

2   Agree together beforehand that having a different perception of an issue does not make either perception wrong.

3   Try not to use the 'you' word. Use the 'I' word whenever possible.

4   Ensure that the reply date or time is realistic.

5   The AS partner often needs more time to think things through, so it might take a little longer.

6   The focus should be on resolution, not provocation, and should not lead to further disagreements.

Unresolved Issues

Unresolved Issues reply

....

....

....

....

....

....

....

....

....

....

....

....

....

Good communication is crucial for any relationship to run smoothly. As NT and AS partners talk different languages, it is inevitable that communication may frequently break down between them. Both need to accept that there is a language difference and work hard at learning how to get it right. Being different does not make either partner wrong. As I have described, they are simply transmitting on a different wave length.

Through practice, understanding will improve as each adjusts to the other's language. It is more likely that the NT partner will be adjusting the most, primarily due to their developed theory of mind allowing them to imagine another's situation. A person blind from birth would find it very difficult to imagine the colour blue, whereas a sighted person does not need to see blue to imagine what the colour blue looks like. It is therefore easier for a person who has the benefit of a fully developed social intelligence and theory of mind to imagine the difficulty not having these skills may bring; in particular the difficulty the AS partner may have in reading non-verbal communication.

Chapter Three

NON-VERBAL COMMUNICATION

Non-verbal communication is responsible for the majority of misunderstandings. Non-verbal communication can be body language, nuance of intonation or physical touch. When describing the importance of non-verbal communication to couples, I outline that often the AS partner will have difficulty reading the NT partner's non-verbal communication. The AS partner may say, 'No one at work has difficulty communicating with me.' The NT partner may say, 'I seem to be the only person my partner cannot (or won't) read.' To the NT partner, the AS partner's difficulty in this area can appear to be selective or biased against them. There are reasons for this. It may also seem that problems have become worse the longer the relationship has gone on.

When we communicate with people we have recently met or we only know on a superficial level, we rely heavily on verbal communication, going into detail to explain what we mean. For example, communication at work is likely to be work related. It is more than likely that the AS partner will know exactly what is being discussed; they may even be an expert on the subject. This form of communication is far removed from the type shared by long-term partners.

Over the course of time each partner will learn much about the other's ways – hence statements like:

- 'You know me inside out.'

- 'I only have to look at you and I know what you are thinking.'

- 'I am just being me – you know that.'

- 'How could you even think that after so long?'

- 'Surely you know me by now?'

The list is endless, but the one thing that all these statements suggest is that there is an assumption by one that the other can read their mind, so to speak, thus obviating the need to be explicit about what is actually going on in their own mind. These assumptions grow over the couple's time together and, particularly in an NT/AS relationship, these assumptions may develop into misunderstandings.

Assumptions

Being aware of these growing assumptions between them is very important for the couple. It is probably not something they have ever asked one another about. The AS partner will probably be quite unaware of the NT partner's nuance of body language in a given situation, while the NT partner will have presumed it has been understood. The AS partner's lack of or inappropriate response is likely to cause the NT partner to take it as a sign of not caring or of not being bothered on the part of the AS partner.

For example, our AS partner makes coffee for them both and they sit down to drink it together. Our NT partner gives the AS partner a tender look of 'thank you'. Our AS partner doesn't quite understand and looks blankly back, which our NT partner misunderstands as there being something wrong. Our NT partner assumed that our AS partner understood the look to mean 'thank you'. Our AS partner, a bit confused, thought they had done something wrong.

With couples I encourage the AS partner, whenever they find themselves unsure about something, to ask the NT partner what a look means or what they are thinking. I recommend that in response to this the NT partner might ask back what they thought they were thinking. In this way the couple can begin to discover what is really going on and not develop further assumptions. This sounds simple but it can make such a difference. Checking that assumptions are correct or not can have a very positive effect on thoughts and feelings that may otherwise have been left in a negative state. Additionally, the AS partner may have stored the look their NT partner gave them and may recognise it more easily in the future.

It is not unusual for the AS partner to assume that the message they are picking up is negative. This may go back to childhood, especially if they were bullied as a child or misunderstood by others. They have come to assume negative reactions from others. It may be over something they have said, an opinion they have expressed, or the way they have behaved. It is often the negative thoughts and opinions that are expressed more openly, especially in the school playground.

Intonation of communication

When working with couples I constantly check out what has been heard, both by the couple from me and by each from the other. I do not assume that a message has been heard accurately as a critical or negative message may have been received when in fact the opposite was meant. Not being able to read the intonation of a message can cause many misunderstandings. A single sentence can take on many different meanings according to how it is said. For instance, the following four sentences could be compliments:

- 'You *really* do make me laugh.'

- 'You *can* be so caring.'

- 'You *are* such a good listener.'

- 'Your *thoughtfulness* never ceases to amaze me.'

The italics are where the emphasis falls in the intonation but in addition, difficult to convey here, it is how each sentence is spoken. Change the emphasis and the tone of each of the four sentences and they become critical, sarcastic or carry negative connotations:

- 'You really *do* make me laugh!'

- 'You can be *so* caring!'

- 'You are *such* a good listener!'

- 'Your thoughtfulness *never* ceases to amaze me!'

When the ability to interpret the difference between sarcasm, irony or a genuine statement is limited, it is not surprising that misunderstandings arise in communication. An AS partner may not be aware that this difficulty exists for them. They have probably never learned or acquired these subtleties of intonation. Often a negative or literal interpretation is taken when neither is intended. Learning about Asperger syndrome – how it affects an AS partner and how the differences between AS and NT can complicate non-verbal communication – is important. I have set out a way an NT partner can check out how well their AS partner is doing in understanding them. If the couple are both AS, then it will need a third party, possibly a therapist, to do this with you.

This test should be a fun thing for a couple to try out so it is important that it is tried when both partners are feeling good and the relationship is reasonably stable. Remember, you're trying to learn about one another.

Instructions for using the Intonation test

1   Each partner should have a worksheet.

2   The NT partner should read each statement to the AS partner, making a note on their sheet as to whether their intonation is giving a negative or positive message. Remember each statement can mean different things depending upon the intonation.

3   The AS partner should tick the box that they feel is how the statement is meant. For example, if the sentence sounds like sarcasm and therefore negative, then tick the negative box.

4   When the NT partner has read all the statements, work out together how well the AS partner has understood the statements. Try repeating the statements that were not understood correctly again so that the AS partner can perhaps hear the intonation.

AS Intonation test

You make me laugh.

    Positive ☐   Negative ☐

Well that was really clever.

    Positive ☐   Negative ☐

Thank you for thinking of me.

    Positive ☐   Negative ☐

No it's okay – I'll do it.

    Positive ☐   Negative ☐

You just sit there and rest my love.

    Positive ☐   Negative ☐

Have you got a problem with that?

    Positive ☐   Negative ☐

What did you say?

    Positive ☐   Negative ☐

Are you okay to do that?

    Positive ☐   Negative ☐

You really hit the jackpot with that one.

    Positive ☐   Negative ☐

Where did you get that dress/shirt?

    Positive ☐   Negative ☐

The more the NT partner understands how their AS partner's brain works, how their partner reads both them and others, the fewer misunderstandings there will be. Likewise the AS partner has to appreciate that they do not always read a situation correctly, so when they do feel unsure or criticised about a look or something their partner has said, it is important that the AS partner asks.

Working on the non-verbal side of the relationship will not be easy if the AS partner is sensitive to perceived criticism and unable to ask their partner when they feel that criticism. The NT partner is likely not to be aware that the AS partner has perceived something they said as critical. The NT partner should look out for these signs, such as a blank look, that might suggest misinterpretation and check it out with their partner.

In the coffee example I encouraged our AS partner to ask the NT partner why they had looked at them in a certain way. However, maybe when our NT partner received a blank stare they could have verbalised how they were feeling a little. It's about being aware of these signs and not letting them go by unchecked.

The AS partner will believe that if the NT partner says something, then that is what the NT partner means. It will not occur to the AS partner that there is a hidden meaning within the intonation. The Intonation test should help the couple to appreciate how this happens.

How can this pattern be changed? If this has become a major concern and the couple find it difficult to stop and ask, they may need to work this through with a therapist. Learning about this absence of non-verbal skills from a third party, especially if the relationship is struggling, may be received better by the AS partner. To identify what it is that has been misread will require the couple to pause the conversation, usually as soon as something appears to have been misunderstood. There may be that blank look on the AS partner's face, telling the NT partner that something may not have been understood correctly, or the AS partner may abruptly disengage and walk away. Whichever way it is, the NT partner is more likely to sense this and may even have witnessed it many times.

MAD moments

I call these moments when a misunderstanding has occured MAD: (Misread And Dodgy) moments. They need to be verbalised with one partner saying, 'I think this is a MAD moment.' The NT partner is likely to be best equipped to identify these moments. Having called for a 'time-out' to identify the misunderstanding, communication should be on a direct and clear line where both take their turn to speak, respecting one another's right to have their say. The following are a few rules I recommend using when a MAD moment is called.

RULES FOR

Misread And Dodgy (MAD) moments

- *IDENTIFICATION* (EITHER): A look, a comment, an uncomfortable feeling, walking away.

- *PAUSE* (EITHER): Achieved by saying, 'I think this is a MAD moment.'

- *SPEAKING UP* (AS): Saying what has been heard without interruption.

- *EXPLAINING* (NT): Saying what was meant in what was said and the true meaning behind it.

- *UNDERSTANDING* (AS): Repeating back what has been explained and saying if it is now understood.

- *REPEATING* (NT): If necessary stating again what was meant.

- *ACCEPTING* (BOTH): Confirming the true meaning is now understood and accepting this was a MAD moment.

- *INTERRUPTING* (BOTH): not allowed by either at any time.

MAD moments can occur at any time, whether the couple are in private or public situations. MAD moments in public can be harder to prevent and rectify so other strategies have to be put into place. This brings us to our next important chapter, which focuses on socialising and social events.

Chapter
Four
SOCIAL INTERACTION

AS partners often tell me about feeling uncomfortable in social situations but not being able to determine why they have this feeling. Bearing in mind that Asperger syndrome causes difficulties with reading social signals or appreciating when to leave some things unsaid, this feeling of being uncomfortable may not be too uncommon for them. Sometimes an AS partner may be accused of being unfeeling or tactless in their delivery of an opinion or an event. It is said of people with AS that they cannot lie. However, this is not a moral honesty; it is a straight-forward delivery of a statement, often without any diplomacy. For instance, I always warn NT partners not to ask questions like 'What do you think of my new hairdo?' or 'Does my bottom look big in these jeans?' if they do not want the absolute brutal truth. NT partners become familiar with this and understand their partner is not being cruel if something uncomplimentary is said. Some even take comfort in the knowledge that their partner will always tell them what they mean and not offer false flattery.

However, other people the couple encounter in a social context do not have the benefit of this knowledge and will often be taken aback by the AS partner's brutal honesty. If they make the mistake of asking a question or seeking an opinion, they may get an answer they were not prepared for. NT partners sometimes notice the warning signs that their partner is about to say or do something inappropriate. I often suggest that the couple arrange a way for the NT partner to signal to their partner not to say it, to keep quiet and not to follow their natural impulses. This could be done with a little pinch, a cough or squeeze of the arm. If this is prearranged it can save many potential embarrassing moments and can even be amusing later, when the couple discuss what happened while they were out. Having Asperger syndrome is not an excuse to be rude, unintentionally or not. Hurting someone else's feelings is not nice; it is as simple as that and has to be clearly understood.

Putting together specific rules for socialising can make a difference. Having prearranged agreements and strategies in place can help prevent difficult or embarrassing moments in the future. I have made a list of some of the issues that are often raised within counselling sessions. This may help you construct your own list.

Important socialising rules

- If I pinch you, it means stop saying what you are saying immediately.

- If I wink at you, it means you are doing really well.

- If I ask you 'Do you remember what you wanted to say to me?' it means change the subject and I will explain later.

- If you are feeling overloaded by the situation or becoming tired, say to me, 'I think I have a migraine coming on.' We can then excuse ourselves from the situation.

- If you feel the impulse to just leave or go home, you must tell me or send a text. Otherwise I will feel abandoned by you. I will not be cross but I will need to know where you are or how I can get home.

- If we are with other people, including family, and you take a dislike to their children, pet, partner, family, friends, clothes, car, job or hobby, please do not say so. We can discuss it alone later. They do not need to know of your dislike.

Instructions for filling in your Important Socialising Rules worksheet

1   Take time together when you are not going to be disturbed.

2   Make sure the AS partner understands that in many situations you are their social guide and your only intention is to save both of you embarrassment or avoid arguments.

3   Think about past cases when things have gone wrong or where there was an embarrassing situation.

4   Think how this could have been prevented.

5   Put together a list of strategies and rules that you can both work to.

6   When you have finished, check that the AS partner is not feeling put down or inferior in any way.

7   Remember you both have different talents and it is unlikely that socialising will be the AS partner's forte, just as logical processes are not necessarily yours.

8   When it is completed, put copies up on the wall so the rules can be rehearsed and remembered. Revisit the list before a social event.

9   Start to put the rules into place as soon as possible. Practise in order for them to become part of your routine when out together in company.

Our Important Socialising Rules list

....

....

....

....

....

....

....

....

....

....

....

....

When it comes to socialising, remember that word 'difference'. In Chapter 1 I used the analogy of an eagle and a zebra trying very hard to work with their differences. They had fallen in love with each other and wanted to live together. I talked about needing a different type of food, one being carnivorous and the other herbivorous. The other difference I mentioned was the need for a different environment to live in. Eagle likes a solitary habitat far away from crowds, whereas Zebra, a herding animal, needs to be surrounded by others they can interact with.

A need for a different environment

A relationship between an AS and NT partner is not so different from Eagle and Zebra in respect of feeding and environment. The NT partner will tend to require that emotional food found in acknowledgement of them, hugging and touching or intangible, subtle expressions of devotion. The AS partner will need the logical food found in their work, business or special interests. For the majority of NT partners, living a solitary existence would be difficult, perhaps leaving them with feelings of social isolation. Likewise for an AS partner to spend too much time in group situations, trying to be sociable, will also be very difficult and quickly use up their available resources, leading to possible meltdown.

I described earlier how the AS brain is trying to work out people and communication using logic; how this leads to their brain working many times harder than a person who has a fully developed theory of mind. Their resources will be quickly depleted in social and group situations, as they try to figure what they are supposed to say and do, as well as what the other people around them are going to say and do. To expect the partner with AS to be able to keep up to speed in social communication and situations would only end in both feeling disappointed and let down. This is why such a major difference needs to be recognised, accepted and openly discussed, in order for both partners to spend time in their own essential environments, either alone or with others, and not feel guilty or abandoned because of it.

Difference can work, but only if the couple is aware of how it affects them and their relationship. This way the expectations of either partner will not exceed the reality. Sometimes socialising for an AS/NT couple is not a problem because either neither of them enjoy socialising or the NT partner has already recognised their separate need for social contact and is happy to fulfil this alone, without expecting their partner to participate. This decision can be quite difficult for some NT partners as they would really prefer that their partner shared this with them;

very much in the same way their AS partner would like them to share or take part in their special interest. Some NT partners I have discussed this with say how guilty they feel leaving their partner alone, or how they feel obligated to leave an event early as their AS partner wants to go. My answer is always to say that their AS partner would actually be far happier left alone to freely pursue what interests them and not have to feel guilty for doing this either. The NT partner needs to recognise their AS partner does not need to share the same environment – they will not benefit in any way from doing so – and to work with this difference.

However, it is often at special times like birthdays, Christmas and anniversaries when the need to share and celebrate the occasion together is important to the NT partner. The AS partner needs to be aware of this and ensure they make a special effort at these special times so their NT partner is not left feeling unloved and neglected.

Celebrations

Some NT partners have reported not receiving a card, let alone a present, and this seems even more likely to happen if the AS partner is male. This may be due to upbringing; perhaps cards, presents and celebrating special occasions were not part of the AS partner's childhood. Another reason may be because they are not particularly bothered about receiving anything, so find it difficult to appreciate why anyone else would want to receive these things.

One reason people give gifts and cards is because the other person's happiness makes them happy. The very act of giving, even if the gift or card is not to the receiver's taste, does please. Due to a lack of theory of mind, the AS partner will tend to struggle to figure out what their partner wants to receive and may become anxious over getting it right. This need to get it right can be the very reason why the AS partner does not buy anything; the fear of getting it wrong may be so strong that they will not buy anything at all. The AS partner may find it very hard to imagine what it is their partner would like to receive. Trying to think of presents and surprises can be nigh on impossible for the AS partner.

When I discuss this with clients, the AS partner will often say, 'Why can't they [partner] just say what they want and I can just go and get it?' This is a very logical solution to the problem. However, it does not suit all NT partners who then feel deprived of the emotional aspect of a surprise gift. For the NT partner receiving gifts is an emotional experience as well as a practical one. NT partners can feel valued if their partner has put some effort and time into the gift and the surprise is always a pleasure.

By the same token, having the NT partner turn around and say 'I'd like a bracelet for my birthday' is potentially a timebomb for the AS partner. It will be a source of great stress and anxiety as the AS partner will be unable to imagine what kind of bracelet their partner would like. Torment over what the NT partner expects the bracelet to be like, or how much money it should cost will ensue.

Special occasions can be a source of anxiety, stress and hurt feelings for both partners. There is a way round this that I have developed and found to be quite successful. The NT partner needs to give their AS partner a list of, let's say, ten things they'd like to receive, any of which would be a pleasure to have. This way the AS partner will know exactly what to get and the NT partner will still have the surprise of not knowing what will be chosen from the list. I have set out some examples and then a blank copy of a birthday, Christmas and anniversary sheet. If you belong to a culture that has different celebrations which involve giving gifts, then there is a blank sheet for you to fill in.

Instructions for filling in the present list – for the NT partner

1   Complete the appropriate list at least one month before the date of the celebration.

2   Be sure that all gifts are equally desired.

3   Be very accurate with the present, where to buy, colour, size, etc., and above all be clear about the price range. You could put, say, no more than £25 or between £10 and £15.

4   Do not under any circumstances say after the event that you wish something else had been chosen from the list.

Instructions for buying the present from the list – for the AS partner

1   Choose one (or more) of the presents you would like to buy your partner.

2   Take time to be sure you have read the list accurately.

3   Make sure you hide the present in a safe place.

4   Do not give any clues as to what the present is.

5   Disguise the present when you wrap it, so your partner will not be able to guess what it is, for instance, put it in a bigger box.

6   Take time to choose some nice paper and a card.

7   Write a nice message on the card.

BIRTHDAY PRESENTS

Present

Where to buy it ....

Price ....

Size/type/colour ....

Present

Where to buy it ....

Price ....

Size/type/colour ....

Present

Where to buy it ....

Price ....

Size/type/colour ....

Present

Where to buy it ....

Price ....

Size/type/colour ....

CHRISTMAS PRESENTS

Present

Where to buy it ....

Price ....

Size/type/colour ....

Present

Where to buy it ....

Price ....

Size/type/colour ....

Present

Where to buy it ....

Price ....

Size/type/colour ....

Present

Where to buy it ....

Price ....

Size/type/colour ....

ANNIVERSARY PRESENTS

Present

Where to buy it ....

Price ....

Size/type/colour ....

Present

Where to buy it ....

Price ....

Size/type/colour ....

Present

Where to buy it ....

Price ....

Size/type/colour ....

Present

Where to buy it ....

Price ....

Size/type/colour ....

PRESENTS FOR OTHER OCCASIONS

Present

Where to buy it ....

Price ....

Size/type/colour ....

Present

Where to buy it ....

Price ....

Size/type/colour ....

Present

Where to buy it ....

Price ....

Size/type/colour ....

Present

Where to buy it ....

Price ....

Size/type/colour ....

These sorts of lists can take a tremendous pressure off the AS partner as all the guesswork and risk of failure are removed. The NT partner still has the element of surprise as they won't know which gift their partner has chosen. The majority of AS partners I see say they just want to make their partner happy. Unfortunately, many do not know how, but at least knowing what their partner would like as a gift can make such a difference to them both. Using specific lists like these can make happy occasions happier.

It is really important that the NT partner does not feel impolite or selfish about the items listed. It might take time to get used to doing this as it is often easier to give than receive. It really does make things so much easier for the AS partner. Both will gain from the removal of the pressure of choosing and the fear of disappointing. These lists can also be given to the AS partner to fill in, as in some cases the NT partner will also find it a struggle to predict what will be an appropriate gift to make their AS partner happy.

Arranging surprise celebrations

The other area where lists can prove useful is in arranging surprise evenings out. Many NT clients have stated that they feel responsible for making all the social arrangements; that if they did not arrange things they would never go anywhere. This can leave the NT partner feeling, once again, unloved and undervalued. They often yearn for their partners to do something for them and to show they are important enough to spoil every now and then. Not a lot to ask, you may think. However, once again the decision of what to choose – fearing they might disappoint – makes it very difficult for the AS partner. Basically the AS partner needs to know what their NT partner would like to do. Without directions it is unlikely that the AS partner will succeed at this task and the surprise night out which the NT partner desperately wants may not happen. The AS partner may have memories of failed evenings in the past and does not want to risk further confrontation or feelings of failure.

Once again a simple list can help change all this and make a positive difference to both. Below are instructions, followed by an example of a 'places to celebrate' list which the NT partner can fill in. It may also be useful for the AS partner to fill in these lists, in order to maintain a balance in the relationship.

Instructions for filling in the surprise celebrations list – for the NT (or AS) partner

1 Have at least four places on the list at all times.

2 Be sure that any of the places or events is somewhere you would equally like to go.

3 Be accurate about the venue and any special things you like at certain places.

4 Under no circumstances say after the event that you wish something else had been chosen.

PLACES OR EVENTS TO GO TO

Place or event ....

Location ....

Things I like ....

Date or days ....

Place or event ....

Location ....

Things I like ....

Date or days ....

Place or event ....

Location ....

Things I like ....

Date or days ....

Place or event ....

Location ....

Things I like ....

Date or days ....

So much is about finding out what works for you and your family. It is about experimenting, and sometimes trial and error. Making rules and establishing strategies can work wonders in an AS/NT relationship. However, sometimes a new situation comes up where the old strategy needs to be adjusted to fit it. This is called putting things into context.

Getting the context right

Rules and strategies are useful as they work well within an AS/NT relationship. However, no rule can deal with all situations and at times adjustments need to be made. The AS partner may find this difficult as they can tend to be reluctant to make changes. For example, the AS partner does not know when their NT partner wants a hug. The couple may have a rule that if I am crying then that means I want a hug. This is fine until it is something the AS partner has done which has left the NT partner angry and in tears. The AS partner coming over to hug may elicit a sharp response. An adjustment to the rule might be that when the NT partner is crying the AS partner actually says, 'Hug?' before trying to.

Some NT partners complain that their AS partner learns very little from social situations; that they are weary of continually reinforcing the learning and adapting to new situations. Unfortunately there is little that can be done about this. The NT partner will in many ways be the social guide in the relationship. I try to put this in perspective by asking, 'If your partner was visually impaired, would you expect them to automatically know where things were in an unfamiliar environment?' Looking at it this way helps improve the understanding of why things happen as they do. This is not due to the AS partner's reluctance to try; it is due to being affected by Asperger syndrome which makes certain things difficult to achieve. This does not excuse the AS partner from trying to learn or adapt to situations they find themselves in – quite the contrary. If the NT partner sees efforts being made, even if those efforts are not quite right, the feeling of being alone is eased. Maintenance of the relationship should not be left entirely up to the NT partner.

In most cases this news is welcomed by the AS partner, who wants to feel they can participate in making improvements and take some of the responsibility for the relationship. This can be especially true when it comes to the sexual relationship the couple share.

Chapter
Five
SEXUAL ISSUES

This is an area that seems either to work very well or is fraught with difficulties for AS/NT relationships. If you fall into the former category then this chapter may not be applicable to you. The most common comments given by NT partners are of feeling either sexually used or sexually deprived. They talk about feelings of not being desired, being undervalued and that their partner is no longer attracted to them. There is a greater prevalence of this when the AS partner is male and the NT partner is female.

Making each other feel good and acknowledging the positives each brings are all part of building intimacy. When I ask the AS adult what he values about his partner, he will often proceed to tell me what they do or how they look rather than relating it to who their partner is. For example, rather than telling his partner she does a good job looking after the children, he could say to her, 'You are a really good mother.' Starting with the words 'You are' can completely change the relevance of the statement.

Sex is a form of communication and, as we already know, this can be difficult for the AS partner. Getting the timing right, trying to read their partner's sexual signals or figuring out what is wanted are all a bit of a struggle. Sometimes the AS partner may decide that because they feel like making love then their partner must do too. Again this is due to lack of theory of mind, the inability to appreciate that someone can have a different mind set to their own.

Using colours or a traffic light system works quite well: for instance, green can mean yes I want you; amber, I am thinking about it, let's see what happens; and red means no I would just like a cuddle tonight. A colour for desire can also be agreed between the couple. For instance, say the colour is purple, it can then be added to the feelings in colour system I discussed on pp. 29–35. Each could then indicate their sexual desire through saying something like, 'My colour purple is eight tonight. What's yours?' A word of warning here. It is important with either the traffic lights or the level of the desire colour that neither partner feels pressurised or rejected by their partner's response. At all times, whatever the outcome, the couple should try and cuddle.

Another way is to use an obvious, mutually agreed sign such as for the NT partner to say, 'If I take my nightdress off or place your hand on my breast, I really desire you and making love would be nice.' Again it must be agreed that this does not mean they have to make love. If the couple are not sharing the same sexual desire, it will be just as lovely to cuddle one another.

Another problem NT partners express is a feeling that they have a low libido because they are not wooed by their partner or made to feel physically special. I have heard NT women say, 'Why would I want to make love to someone who's barely said two words to me all day?' Of course we're back to the same problem of our AS partner not knowing what they are supposed to say or do. Knowing what to do or when to do it can be a major problem for our AS partner. They also tend to worry about getting things wrong. However, on the obverse, the NT partner does not want to have to tell their partner what to do at the time. This would result in even more feelings of not being special.

Making a partner feel special

I have compiled a short list of suggestions that the AS partner could use to make the NT partner feel wooed. Obviously making your own list will make the suggestions more personal and special. Use the list to make one another feel special.

You could even designate specific days to each other. In this way, our AS partner will know when it is their turn to do something special.

- Say something nice about your partner's physical appearance or attire.

- Bring home flowers, a rose, a plant, a gift.

- Include a little card that you have written a nice message on.

- Give or post your partner a card to say how much you appreciate them.

- Run a nice hot bath and put some oils or a fragrant bubble bath in it.

- Light some candles in the bathroom to make it even more romantic.

- Candles and turning lights down are always romantic and set the scene for intimacy.

- Give your partner a back and neck massage. Spend time over this and use fragrant oils.

- Tell your partner you love them, even if you have already told them this before or earlier in the day.

- Try and tell them the things you love them for.

Instructions for filling in the Wooing list

1 Make some time together to fill out a list.

2 Being in bed together, maybe on a Sunday morning, can be a good time.

3 Both think of ideas you would like to do or have your partner do that would make you feel loved, desired and valued.

4 You can have a list each or combine your lists together.

Our Wooing list

You will need to experiment until you find what works for you. Sometimes the sexual side of a relationship can be a real problem due to the AS partner being affected by sensory sensitivity. This may be more likely when the AS partner is female.

Sensory sensitivity

Sensory sensitivity can present itself in various forms. It can affect any of the senses – sight, hearing, smell, taste and touch. Sometimes the AS partner may not realise they are affected, presuming that everyone else is the same. This can result in them not talking about how something makes them feel, presuming their partner already knows.

One male NT partner told me how his female AS partner would push him away whenever he tried to touch her breasts. He assured me that his partner's breasts were beautiful and he had told her so. He also added that he was very gentle. What he did not realise was that to his partner this gentle touching was irritating and unpleasant. Sensory sensitivity can cause an extreme, almost painful reaction to being touched in a specific way in specific places. This can be any part of the body. However, the most common areas for women are the nipples, clitoris, arms and ears. For some AS men it can be the penis, and it may be painful for them when they climax or irritating if touched in a certain way.

Sometimes the problem is the way in which one partner actually touches the other. Often it is the gentle, tickling, stroking movements that can cause the most extreme reaction, and the longer this goes on, the worse it can feel. Ask the AS partner to demonstrate how they would touch themselves. Learn from this, practise and be guided by them. It is their body, after all, and they will be the expert on how they like to be touched. Finding a way to touch that does not cause such a reaction, or restricting touch to safe parts of the body, can eliminate this problem.

NT partners may feel this is depriving them, as the part of the body that they're asked not to touch is the part that gives them sexual arousal, such as the nipples or the breasts. I often ask them to imagine how it would feel to have their penis or nipples rubbed with wire wool. This normally gets the message across. Sensory sensitivity is very real for the AS partner. It is important to respect this and not force change that could upset or alienate.

Smell and taste can also be affected. I have worked with AS partners, in particular AS women, who find their partners' bodily fluids repulsive and find oral sex, or even in some cases kissing, almost impossible. Sometimes the problem can be remedied if their partner cleans their teeth or has a bath. It is something that needs discussion and experimentation in an effort to find a compromise without it becoming confrontational. Confrontation could result in non-disclosure and an avoidance of sex altogether.

Making love is about pleasing one another and few caring partners would want to put their loved one through something they clearly did not enjoy. It is important to find out what affects the AS partner and not to make them feel guilty for their sensory sensitivity.

I have put together a list of the most common effects. Read through the list together and identify any that the AS partner is affected by. Some of the issues on the list are of a very sensitive nature and would probably be quite difficult to discuss, especially in the early stages of a relationship. If it is felt that these issues may be too embarrassing or sensitive to talk about alone, then try to find a therapist to discuss them with. Be sure to find someone who is familiar with both Asperger syndrome and how it can affect sensory sensitivity.

Sensory sensitivity and sex

Sight

- Having lights on that are too bright.

- Being in the dark.

Hearing

- Having the television, radio or any background noise on, including romantic music.

- Whispering or breathing in the partner's ear.

Smell

- Some fragrances can be abhorrent. Make sure your perfume or fragrant candles are not unpleasant to your partner.

- Oral sex could be very unpleasant for the AS partner with a sensitive sense of smell. Washing first might solve this.

- Give your partner permission to say if your breath is not pleasant to them. Maybe a breath freshener would solve this.

Taste

- Oral sex could be very unpleasant for the AS partner due to the taste. Washing first might solve this.

Touch

- Certain parts of the body may be oversensitive to touch. Find out what these are and the best way to touch your partner.

- Certain parts of the body may be undersensitive to touch. For some AS men this could be the penis. He may sometimes find it is only possible to reach an orgasm through masturbation, either by himself or by his partner.

- Certain fabrics can be irritating or unpleasant for the AS partner, such as nightclothes or sheets.

Finding a new way of sexual communication

Experimentation and the ability to discuss the sexual side of the relationship openly are important. This might be quite difficult to do for some partners, especially if using sexual language and terms is something a couple are not used to or feel uncomfortable with. Finding a substitute name for a sexual part of the body can really make a difference to this as it allows a couple to discuss parts of their bodies as though in the third person. For example, both the vagina and the penis could be personalised with names such as Daisy and Dennis. It might feel easier to say, 'Daisy is fast asleep and doesn't think she can wake up' as opposed to 'Sorry but I am far too tired to make love tonight.' Or it could work to say 'Dennis has fallen asleep after a long day.' A sense of fun can develop from this. One partner could touch the other and say, 'Oh, Dennis is feeling a bit frisky tonight!'

The aim is to bring the fun into sex. This is something that seems to get lost in some AS/NT relationships, often due to not knowing what to say for fear of getting it wrong or hurting the other's feelings. Using pet names and giving sexual parts personalities can allow communication not to take on a personal or clinical tone. It also allows couples to find out whether their partner wants to make love or wants to be close, but not necessarily have an orgasm. For example, he could ask her whether Daisy wants to come out to play. She might say, 'Daisy would love Dennis to visit but he's not to worry about making her come.'

A whole new language can develop between the couple. Pet names can be given for other parts of the body too such as the breasts and testicles. It is creative and makes sex fun, imaginative and playful. Once again this will not work for every couple, but when it does work it seems to work well. Decide together if you feel it will work for you. Experiment, choose names, explore with the language you use. Sex should be both a physical pleasure and fun. It should be unrestricted while maintaining respect and trust. Find what works for you. Making love is what makes you a couple. Maybe think back to how it used to be when you first met. It is sad that for some couples the fun and intimate closeness are lost in time. This can be due to changes in the roles of the couple, from partner to parent, or even stepparent.

Chapter
Six

PARENTING

As well as being a partner, the AS partner is very often a parent too. This brings a new set of variables to the couple's life together. Being a parent is not easy at the best of times and being a parent affected by Asperger syndrome can be even more difficult. An AS parent will struggle with a child's development and the way children constantly change. If there is more than one child then this will mean being aware of multiple differences in ability and understanding of each child's development.

An example I use to highlight this is a seven-year-old girl who asked her AS dad to help her with some arithmetic homework. Dad was pleased. Being an accountant meant this was something of his forte. However, instead of dealing with the arithmetic in hand he took it upon himself to try and teach his daughter some very complex equations he believed would help her understand arithmetic better. It was not long before the girl was in tears and he was frustrated. For her the equations were beyond her stage of learning. For him he didn't realise she was too young to grasp such equations. When the mother became involved it turned into a row between the couple. The upshot of it all was that the very upset little girl would probably not ask for her father's help again.

What has happened relates to lack of theory of mind on the father's part, whose expectations of his daughter's cognitive capacity were far beyond her ability. He did not understand the developmental stage for her age. He did not intend to upset his daughter and was probably at a loss as to why she had become upset. He would have then felt he had got it wrong, or was being unfairly got at, when his intentions were to help his daughter.

Incidents like this occur in many different forms; it may be at the dinner table over table manners and etiquette, where expectations may be far above what the child is capable of. Dropping crumbs, keeping clothes clean or not making a mess are all potential risk situations. The AS parent may become irritated and frustrated with the child for dropping a drink on the floor and their reaction may sometimes be out of context to the extent of the accident.

Being distracted

Another danger area is the AS parent becoming distracted or not seeing the potential consequences of their behaviour. Examples of this include accounts of children being left alone because the AS parent had become distracted by something they saw as being more important. The AS partner isn't being neglectful; they merely think the child is more developed than they are.

A couple related the following to me. Before leaving for work, the NT parent asked their AS partner to pick up a prescription from the chemist. The AS partner only remembered about this 15 minutes before the chemist was due to close. By the time the two children had been dressed and strapped into their car seats, they would have been too late for the chemist. Rather than let their partner down and maybe have a confrontation, the AS partner left the children watching television and dashed out to the shop. Meanwhile the NT parent returned to find the six- and four-year-old alone and distressed. The NT parent was furious with their partner upon their return. Tempers flared and many hurtful things were said. The AS partner had not anticipated the consequences both to themselves and to the children.

Occurrences such as these will undermine the trust of the NT parent in their partner's capacity to take care of the children. This can affect the whole family and it is likely that the NT parent will become very protective and defensive of the children, resulting in the AS parent feeling isolated and criticised. Some AS parents decide not to be involved with their children's upbringing and distance themselves from the family. They may decide not to take part in any of the decisions involving the childcare and leave the NT parent with total responsibility for the children. This distancing works for some couples, but for the majority of couples, where trust does break down, the AS parent is left feeling on the outside and rejected, while the NT parent feels abandoned by the AS partner's apparent irresponsibility. This will not create a happy environment in which to bring up the children.

When I am working with parents affected by Asperger syndrome, I teach them about their children and specific rules that can never be broken under any circumstances. One aspect of this teaching is to educate them about how a child develops and what might be expected at specific ages. There is much written about this and plenty of information on the internet. Although development does not always follow a strict process, it is a rough guide as to what a child may or may not be capable of.

Understanding the kids

Learning about their child's developmental stages can encourage a better understand for the AS parent. Liane Holliday Willey (2000) talks about this in a video presentation with Professor Tony Attwood. Liane describes how she came to realise that she did not understand her neurotypical children. She decided that she needed to do something about this in order to provide the best care she could. Liane read books about neurotypical children. Her descriptions are very much the same as what a neurotypical parent might do where their children are affected by Asperger syndrome. It is about learning what the differences are and working with them rather than against them.

House rules

Another worthwhile strategy for maintaining family harmony is to put together a list of house rules. This can be done between the couple or, if the children are old enough, with the whole family. If rules are agreed upon and made known, then everyone will know what they are doing and misunderstandings may be avoided. It is important that all should have a fair say in what the house rules are to be and they should be agreed between the couple or with the children if old enough.

To keep this fair I recommend that each family member involved has a piece of paper and pen to compile their own personal list of the house rules that would be important to them. Once everyone has completed their list, they should come together and compare them and negotiate what the important rules are. This will require compromise by everyone. If the children are too young or not able to decide for themselves, then it may be more appropriate if the parents or caregivers do this without involving the children.

Example of a list of house rules

House rules for the Smith family

Everyone	If it is your mess then you clean it up.
Everyone	If someone is talking then do not interrupt.
Roger and Sally	Bedtime for Roger and Sally is 9.00 pm.
Everyone	Clothes to be washed must be put in the laundry basket.
Roger	The hamster cage will be cleaned every Saturday.
Roger and Sally	The television will remain off until homework is finished.
Dad	Make sure the dog is taken for a walk every evening.
Mum	Not to give tasks to do or expect a conversation when an important football match is on (unless urgent).

Instructions for making a list together of your family's house rules

1   Arrange a time that all the family can be sat together around a table if possible.

2   Give at least 24 hours' notice for this.

3   Ask each family member to think about the house rules they would like to see in place and to whom the house rule should apply.

4   Each person should bring his or her prepared list to the meeting.

5   Each should be allowed to take it in turns to read their list to the rest of the family (no more than five minutes).

6   There should be a vote on which rules are to be accepted.

7   If it is a draw, then discuss how the rule might be reapplied to suit all concerned.

8   If the children are too young to participate, then the couple can choose five rules each.

9   The rules should be reasonable and offer some benefit to the family.

10   No silly or overcontrolling rules like Dad should always give me a lift, or the children will never leave any of their dinner.

WORKSHEET

	House rules for the .... family

Sharing responsibilities

Often the NT parent will tell me that they feel as if they are looking after an extra child; that they are taking responsibility for the whole relationship and family. In my research (Aston 2003a) I found that many NT partners were originally attracted to the childlike qualities they sensed in their AS partners. For many this was very appealing in the early stages of the relationship. However, what they found as the relationship progressed was that their partner never grew up and remained a bit of a 'Peter Pan'.

An extra child

It may not have been until the children were born that this was noticed. Instead of having a partner sharing the practical and emotional responsibilities of bringing up children, they have a partner who is competing for their attention, as a sibling might do. In fact sibling rivalry is an appropriate term in some cases. Again this is due to not being able to perceive a child's developmental level, or that the relationship their partner has with their child is different and cannot be competed with. This may be difficult for the couple to resolve and may be an issue best addressed with a therapist who has an understanding of the effect of being in an AS family.

Chapter Seven

HOME LIFE

Special interests

It would be unlikely that the home life of the family were not in some way affected by the AS partner's special interest. This is also an area where the AS partner may be able to contribute to the family, as it is likely they are an expert on their particular interest. Interests can vary and change over time: they can be work related such as information technology (IT), flying or the railroad; they may be Playstation games, clocks or stamps. Special interests include anything that the AS person expends much time upon and tends to be knowledgeable about. Having a special interest is very important to the person with Asperger syndrome as it can be said to be mood altering. I have learned from my research and from my many AS clients that people with Asperger syndrome have highly active brains, active to the point where turning their brain off can be a problem, causing erratic sleep patterns. Many clients struggle with sleepless nights, waking up early and just lying in bed thinking.

A special interest is an excellent form of distraction and a way of chilling out. It allows the AS brain to focus and become absorbed in something that is stimulating and pleasurable. It is the AS person's way of relaxing, just as the NT partner may call up a friend or go down to the local pub with some friends to watch a match. I have found that when there is no special interest for the AS person they can become depressed and despondent.

For most couples the AS partner's special interest is not a problem. However, it does seem to become a problem when it appears to take over the AS partner's life and conversation. It is then that the NT partner, and probably the rest of the family too, starts to feel neglected and secondary to the special interest. If the interest is work related, then the NT partner may feel they are living with a workaholic. Let's say that politics is their special interest outside work. The NT partner may find that their AS partner is either continually reading about the subject, looking it up on the internet or out campaigning. This is when strategies and mechanisms need to be brought into place for the couple.

Setting time limits can help. However, these need to be discussed and decided between the couple so that it is fair for both of them. If both have interests that is even better. Then a balance in the relationship can be found where both allocate time to their interests. Where the NT partner does not have a specific interest, spending time with friends in an AS-free environment where they are able to communicate on a more emotional level can be beneficial for both.

Making a written timetable, so that it can be referred to, can be better than just relying on verbal agreements. If the timetable is agreed by both, then it becomes a type of contract and will reinforce the fact they need to adhere to it. Not only will the timetable allow each partner time alone, it will also set aside that quality time together that the NT partner desires and the AS partner can learn. Finding an interest they both like is not always easy. Some of the ones that I have found to work are board or card games, music, theatre, cinema, motorcycling, cycling, running, walking, going to the gym, water sports, visiting historical sites. This shared interest can be for very different reasons. The NT partner might find, for example, that a historical building allows them to capture a glimpse of the past or romanticise about the lives of historical figures, while the AS partner may be enthralled by the architecture, its intricacy or the sheer enormity of the building.

Often shared interests are those that do not involve too much communication; certainly motorcycling, theatre, water sports or even running can be enjoyed without having to talk. The only discussion might be after the event in direct reference to the interest in question, which usually suits both partners.

Quality time together is important for both partners. However, although the NT partner may be able to participate or enter the AS partner's world, it is unlikely that the AS partner will be able to come into the NT partner's world, which can result in the NT partner becoming what is often termed a 'Cassandra' (see Chapter 9).

Time awareness

In my research I found that AS partners are either ruled rigidly by the clock or have no awareness of time at all. Both of these characteristics can cause difficulties with child rearing and the NT partner may find they are either being dominated by a time schedule or constantly being let down by their partner's apparent inability to do anything on time, such as collecting the children from school or arriving for a parents' meeting.

If the AS partner has a history of being late or forgetting to turn up to appointments, the NT partner will find they are taking on more and more responsibilities as the ability to trust their partner to do things on time diminishes. With the balance of responsibilities weighing heavily on the NT partner, feelings of being alone and being the carer for everyone, including their partner, will lead to pebbles being added to their bucket. If the AS partner is willing, there are some strategies that can be put into place to help bring some change to this situation. Even with these changes, the NT person, as social guide in the relationship, will still be carrying the majority of responsibilities for childcare, whether the NT parent is the mother or the father.

Dominated by time

Many people affected by Asperger syndrome find safety in being able to control their environment. One way to do this is to develop time-related routines. However, having entered into a long-term relationship, an AS partner does not have the right to impose these routines on their partner. It is a form of domestic abuse and unacceptable. An AS partner may not appreciate that their routines impinge detrimentally upon their partner and children. They may need to hear it from a therapist.

When there are children in the relationship, the AS partner can become draconian with their routines in an effort to control the children; children the AS partner is already struggling to understand or relate to. In some cases, when the AS partner realises this, there will be an effort to change or the NT partner may decide that they are simply not going to be controlled in this way any more and will be learning to say no.

No time awareness

On the other side of the coin, some NT partners describe how their partner just does not seem to be able to plan things such as how long it will take to get ready or how long it will take to arrive somewhere. It is as if the AS person is only able to be on time when it relates to something they are interested in. If it is football and a particular team, they will know exactly when kick-off is. A useful strategy then is to parallel their interest by saying something like 'It will take you until half-time to get to the school meeting' or 'It will take you the length of the Steve Wright radio show to get to the school meeting.' It is very likely that the AS partner will have a mental record of how long their favourite things take, if only to ensure they set aside the time to enjoy them.

Discuss together what it is that you could use to make this work. I have set out an example of a Time Awareness sheet and there is a blank one for you both to fill in together.

Example of Time Awareness sheet

Task	Time to allow
Driving from work to the school.	Favourite programme Radio Four.
We have to leave in 30 minutes.	Watching EastEnders.
Driving from home to the school.	Rugby match half-time.
Meeting me in an hour and three-quarters.	Football match full time.
Driving to pick Sally up from her martial arts class.	Running two miles.
Driving to pick Johnny up from his piano class.	Walking the dog.
I will meet you back here in one hour.	A yoga class.
Get the dinner out of the oven in 40 minutes.	A workout in the gym.

Instructions for filling in the Time Awareness sheet

1   Arrange some quiet time to sit down together to identify relevant tasks.

2   Write a list in the left-hand column on the time sheet.

3   The NT partner will have to identify how much time needs to be allocated to these tasks.

4   Explore together an activity that the AS partner is interested in that takes a similar amount of time to complete, listen to or watch.

5   The NT partner will need to learn to use these representations when arranging with their partner to carry out tasks which are time dependent.

6   Do not be too serious about this. Try and make it fun but above all do not turn it into a task for the AS partner.

Time Awareness

Task	Time to allow

Selective hearing

It is not uncommon for the NT partner to describe how their AS partner seemingly gets stuck on a minor aspect of a discussion. Sometimes the AS partner may say that, in retrospect, they can see they had become stuck on something and should have let it go. However, this does not seem to prevent it from reoccurring when a new situation presents itself. Once this happens the discussion breaks down and can turn into an argument. The NT partner will suggest that their AS partner has selective hearing, that is, picks out from a discussion the bits they want to hear and deliberately ignores the rest. In a sense this is correct. However, it is not deliberate and for many AS people it can be due to their perception of being criticised.

For example, a female NT partner might come in one day from having visited a friend and say, 'Janet showed me the new bathroom her John has just fitted. It's really lovely and makes me wonder about getting an estimate on having ours done.' Innocuous enough, one might say, but the male AS partner may have heard criticism in the first sentence, insofar as she is saying he doesn't do things like that. The second sentence, where she suggests having the bathroom done by someone professional, he may think she is saying that he is not as capable as John and an argument ensues.

These situations are very difficult to predict and very difficult to calm. Our NT partner will not understand why our AS partner has become resentful. If the situation is to be calmed our NT partner needs to remember that this is selective hearing; it is not deliberate. The onus is on them to pause and try and find out what criticism their AS partner thinks they heard.

Getting the priorities right

AS people often have difficulties in seeing what is or is not important and can become fixated on a trivial or minor task. They may have no idea how to prioritise tasks and refuse to leave a job until it is completed, much to the frustration of those around them who may be trying to have more important tasks completed first.

For example, the AS partner has decided to build a made-to-measure bookcase for their book collection. This is no small task but the AS partner is skilful and determined to give it as much attention as possible, as all the books will need to fit neatly into place. Meanwhile, the NT partner has returned home having bought a couple of shrubs for the garden. The NT partner finds it extremely difficult to dig appropriate holes and asks her partner to help. The AS partner, totally engrossed, simply says, 'You'll have to wait till I have finished the book-case!' The NT partner tries to explain that the shrubs need to be planted and it won't take too long. However, he is now annoyed and a bit frustrated at what appears as his partner's nagging. Both partners are now upset and both are seeing it from different perspectives. The NT partner is aggrieved as she feels she works really hard to make the garden nice for both of them. The AS partner is annoyed as this appears like his partner resents the building of the bookcase.

With the difficulty in applying theory of mind, the AS partner is not able to see the importance of planting the shrubs. He also cannot see that the task will not take too long while their bookcase will be a while yet.

The other side of this is when an AS person is unable to prioritise a series of tasks. This can result in the AS person becoming completely overwhelmed at the very thought of what has to be achieved and not actually achieving any of the tasks. They may attempt to begin a task but then become distracted and start another and another, until utter chaos develops. At this point the AS person may walk away and leave everyone else with the task of clearing up.

The central executive area within the brain governs organisational skills. This is explained very well in Tony Attwood's excellent, well-researched book *The Complete Guide to Asperger's Syndrome* (2007). I highly recommend this book to any-one involved with Asperger syndrome. Difficulties within this area of the brain can cause problems in prioritising tasks.

It may even be noted by the family that priority is often given to those tasks the AS person wants to do most, rather than those that are most important. One way to help prioritise tasks is by making a list and using colours to illuminate the importance of the tasks in question. A whiteboard or large piece of paper can be divided into two lists, one written in red and one written in green (see example).

Example of Organising Priorities sheet

High priority (red)	Low priority (green)
Roger to – Fix leaking tap in the bathroom.	Both to – Clean out fishpond.
Roger to – Johnny's bike – inner tube needs replacing.	Roger to – Prune the apple tree.
Mary to – Get a present for Mum's birthday.	Mary to – Sort out drawers in bedroom.
Mary to – Take faulty radio back to shop.	Both to – Choose a new bed together.
Both to – Go to the travel agents to arrange summer vacation.	Roger to – Take coat in to cleaners.
	Mary to – Make a dental appointment for Johnny.

Instructions for filling in the Priorities list

1   Arrange a time when you can sit down together and not be disturbed.

2   Both think about the tasks you need to do.

3   Arrange together which should be given the highest priority.

4   Arrange who is going to do the task or if it is something for both to do.

5   No more than two tasks each plus two tasks for both can be entered on the red side at any time.

6   Write down on whiteboard or large piece of paper.

7   Put this up somewhere prominent.

8   As a task from the red side is completed then a task from the green side can be transferred over to the red.

9   Tasks on the red side must be completed before any task on the green list.

Organising Priorities sheet

High priority (red)	Low priority (green)

As with any of the worksheets in this book, the couple should experiment to discover what works for them. Remember it is a positive to know that it is Asperger syndrome that has been causing these breakdowns or misunderstandings and that neither partner is to blame. Understanding this can make a big difference to the couple, family or friends; but who else to tell?

Chapter Eight

WHO TO TELL
ABOUT ASPERGER

After a diagnosis of Asperger syndrome, the couple may ask or wish to discuss whom they should tell about the diagnosis. Sometimes there may be a difference of opinion between the couple. The AS partner may not want anyone to know for fear that it will be used against them, or that it suggests they are inferior in some way. Others may not care who knows and see it as irrelevant. One client once said to me, 'What does it matter? I am still me!'

The NT partner would often like to tell everyone, for at last they know they are not going mad and it was not their fault that things were breaking down; it was because of Asperger's. Careful consideration needs to be given to this. It is important to respect the wishes of the AS partner, as long as they are being reasonable and considering all involved. My message to clients is to tell only those where some benefit to the couple is to be gained. It is very important that no one suffers as a consequence of knowing, especially the person with the diagnosis.

The first people couples often think of to tell, if there are any, are the children. Obviously this is very dependent on how old the children are and what the circumstances are. It is, however, a point worth discussing in this book. Children of parents affected by Asperger syndrome can often feel they have not been emotionally supported by the AS parent. They will be aware that the parent may have worked to provide them with the material things they need, but they are unlikely to have felt emotionally valued. The children can often feel they are valued for what they do rather than for who they are. Again due to the difficulty in applying theory of mind, the AS parent is unable to see things from their children's perspective. The AS parent will often not be aware that there is something they are not doing for their children. If the children do not know or understand why, they are likely to take it personally and may feel emotionally neglected by the parent, believing it to be intentional.

Understanding why their AS parent behaves the way they do can make a huge difference. Knowing can allow the child to learn how best to communicate with their AS parent and how to recognise the signs that the parent does care very much for them, although this is often expressed in what the parent does rather than any verbal or physical expressions of love.

For example, one AS parent described how much time they gave to transporting their child to and from private music lessons or dance classes. When their child accused them of never being there for them, they were shocked and deeply hurt by this, feeling that all this effort was not valued.

When the child understood Asperger syndrome and how their parent struggled with emotional expression, how their parent had difficulty understanding what was going on in their world, they could appreciate more that it was not about them and it wasn't that their parent was not interested in their thoughts. To have this reinforced by a third party such as a therapist can result in the parent's situation being taken more seriously by the child and allows the child the opportunity to freely express how it makes them feel and explore any questions they might want to ask without fear of hurting anyone's feelings.

Sometimes parents struggle with how to tell children, especially if they are quite young. I suggest it would not be helpful to try to explain Asperger syndrome to a child below the age of six. I have devised a way of explaining Asperger syndrome that I find can work well as it gives a realistic and practical demonstration of how the parent with Asperger syndrome is affected.

A practical way to demonstrate communication difficulties to a child

1   Ask the child to put on a blindfold or to cover their eyes so they cannot see.

2   Give them a big smile.

3   Now ask them to tell you what you are doing with your face?

4   When the child says they cannot see you to say what you are doing, tell them you were giving a big smile.

5   Ask them why they did not smile back.

6   Repeat 2 to 5, but this time stick your tongue out at them.

7   When the child says again they do not know what you were doing, tell them you're sticking your tongue out at them because they did not smile back.

8   Take off the blindfold.

9   Explain to the child that this is what it is like for Mummy/Daddy, saying they cannot tell what you are thinking or how you are feeling unless you tell them clearly in words.

10   Explain this is how things get misunderstood sometimes because Mummy/Daddy has not understood that they were trying to be friendly, took it that they were not being nice and so may not have been nice back.

11   If you have a recent example you can tell the child about, then use it now.

A practical way to explain the effect of social interaction to a child

1   Ask the child to put the blindfold back on.

2   Ask them to have a go at walking across the room (make sure there is nothing dangerous in the way and you are by their side).

3   When they begin to try this, ask them if they would like you to tell them if there is something in front of them.

4   Give them directions in order that they can walk across a room.

5   Take off the blindfold.

6   Explain that this is what it is like when Daddy/Mummy come into a room, especially if there is lots going on.

7   Explain how it is really hard for them to know what is going on, just like it was hard for the child to know what was in their way.

8   Understanding that Mummy/Daddy has this difficulty will mean they can help by explaining what is happening, in the same way the directions helped them across the room.

9   Explain that when you cannot see it will take longer to move around, just like it takes Mummy/Daddy longer to understand what is happening or what you want them to do, if you do not tell them.

10 Explain how if someone could not see, you would not put something in their way that they would not expect, like moving the furniture around and not telling them about it. This can be used to explain how something unpredictable or unexpected can be very difficult for Daddy/Mummy.

11 Explain to the child that this is what it can be like to have Asperger syndrome.

Keep this whole exercise fun while maintaining the importance of it for both the child and the AS parent to understand one another. It is important that as well as understanding the areas that the AS parent may find difficult, the child understands the talents and skills the AS parent has and the contribution they make to the family.

Telling parents

The next people to discuss telling are often the parents and in-laws of the AS partner. The first thing to consider is the age of the parents concerned. If we are talking about someone in their seventies or eighties, then the question needs to be asked: What benefit will there be in telling them? Often there will be none. The next question to ask is whether they need to know. Making a pros and cons list of benefits against disadvantages might help before disclosure.

Bear in mind that since Asperger syndrome is genetic, one or other of the AS partner's parents may be on the spectrum too, which could potentially lead to a total denial of the diagnosis. This denial can be for two reasons: it is possible that because the person is also on the spectrum they do not see their child's behaviour as different from their own; it is also possible that they do not want to contemplate the fact their offspring is affected by what is, to all intents and purposes, seen as a disability.

Sometimes the result of disclosure can be extreme. Often the NT partner finds themselves excluded from the family and not spoken to again, leaving the AS partner in a very difficult position. If there's a likelihood of such an extreme reaction, there is no benefit in disclosure.

Telling friends

Once again ask the questions: What are the benefits? Do they need to know? More often than not it is the NT partner, especially if they are female, who wants to tell their friends. The NT partner will have experienced a level of emotional deprivation and will probably have discussed their situation with close friends, so the diagnosis can be a watershed insofar as they can now rationalise to their friends the situation they have been in. For example, female NT partners often hear from friends, 'He's just behaving like a man' or may be asked by friends, 'Why are you complaining? He really cares about you.' To be able to say, 'This is not male behaviour, it is Asperger syndrome' or 'Yes he does care but there are some things he is not able to give me' can help validate her existence and restore some of her self-esteem.

Think about the possibility that friends or partners of friends may be on the spectrum too. Consider how and who the AS partner relates to amongst friends. People affected by Asperger syndrome socialise very well with people who perhaps share their 'special interest'. Sometimes friends of the NT partner have discovered that their own partners also have Asperger syndrome, so the disclosure has actually helped them. Once again it is something the couple needs to decide together.

Employers and colleagues at work

Deciding to tell one's employer or, for that matter, one's work colleagues is dangerous ground for the AS partner. Try asking a few people if they know what Asperger syndrome is and I think you'll realise how little is known about it. One client I worked with told his employers and found this worked against him. Their perspective of him changed and, due to his employers' lack of understanding, found he was questioned about his capabilities to fulfil certain tasks, thus undermining self-confidence and ultimately leading to losing his job. There was definitely no benefit there.

I have not only worked with AS clients who have difficulties in employment, but I have also worked with some of their employers to very good effect. Asperger syndrome has many benefits for employers. If an employer is made aware of these, the employer more often than not will want to continue the employment.

I have put together a list of the possible benefits and pitfalls of telling others, which I hope will allow the couple to discuss and decide who to tell.

Example of a post-diagnosis Who to Tell list

Person to tell	Benefits	Costs
Dad	Help him to understand himself.	He may feel responsible.
Mum	Help her to understand both her husband and son.	She may feel let down that no one pointed this out to her before (especially professionals).
Older children	Explain why Dad behaves as he does sometimes.	They may worry that they or their future children may be on the spectrum.
Younger children	None.	Too young to understand.
Boss	Possibly result in making some changes at work.	Could result in discrimination.
Best friend	Help her to understand why I get it wrong sometimes.	Might change her perspective of me for the worse.

Instructions for the Who to Tell list

1   Both have a Who to Tell list.

2   Both decide together on all the relevant people that might be told about Asperger syndrome.

3   Enter the person's name on each list.

4   Fill in the Costs and Benefits columns separately.

5   Compare together what each of you have written down.

6   Decide together who would gain from being told.

Post-diagnosis Who to Tell list

Person to tell	Benefits	Costs

The terminology or wording when telling someone about a diagnosis is important. For example, rather than saying 'I have Asperger syndrome', which suggests that you've caught something, say 'I am affected by Asperger syndrome', which is like saying 'Strong light affects my eyes.' The latter tends to retain who the person is and does not label them so much. I emphasise in my work that Asperger syndrome only affects a small part of the brain; it does not change a person's personality. Their hopes, their dreams, their desires remain the same as most other people's. If a person has the potential to be good at something, they may be even better at it because of being affected by Asperger syndrome. If there was something they were potentially not good at, then likewise they will be less good at it as they will not see the point in trying hard at something they do not enjoy.

Just as it is important to recognise that Asperger syndrome will not take away a person's identity or change who they are, it is equally important to recognise that living with a partner with Asperger syndrome may affect the self-identity of the non-AS partner. This effect is called Cassandra.

Chapter Nine

WHAT IS CASSANDRA?

Cassandra is becoming a recognised term that refers to the NT partner, parent, sibling or child of a person affected by Asperger syndrome. The term Cassandra comes from Greek mythology. Cassandra was a mortal who became the focus of the god Apollo's romantic intentions. In an effort to win the love of the beautiful Cassandra, he gave her the gift of foresight. However, when Cassandra rejected Apollo's romantic intentions, he cursed her by making it so that no one would ever believe the things she told them. This feeling of not being believed is typical of how many NTs feel when living with a person with undiagnosed Asperger syndrome.

Over the years the terminology for the effect of Cassandra has changed. Before Cassandra it was referred to as the mirror syndrome by the Families of Adults Affected by Asperger Syndrome (FAAAS) and then referred to as the Cassandra phenomenon (Rodman 2003). Terminology has since progressed from Cassandra affective disorder and now more appropriately Cassandra affective. The Cassandra phenomenon was first made public at the Families of Adults Affected by Asperger's Syndrome (FAAAS) conference in 2003 as Cassandra affective disorder (CAD) (Aston 2003b) and finally Cassandra affective deprivation disorder (CADD) (Aston 2007).

CADD does not discriminate and can affect the NT person at any age, whether they are male or female and regardless of whether the relationship be heterosexual, homosexual or lesbian. CADD is a secondary disorder and based upon the situation a person is in. It is transitional as it is a consequence of the relationship and is not a personality disorder. Emotional reciprocity, love and belonging are essential human needs. If these needs are not being met and the reason why is not understood, mental and physical health may be affected.

CADD is the result of emotional deprivation due to the fact that one partner, affected by Asperger syndrome, is unable to provide the emotional support the NT partner needs to stay healthy within the relationship. An important point that needs to be made clear is that this effect on the NT partner is rarely intentional on the part of the AS partner. The AS partner is often shocked and saddened when they realise how the relationship is affecting their loved one/s. It is often the little things in the Asperger relationship that can over time cause the most damage. Often when the NT partner tries to explain these things to a friend or therapist, they find themselves apologising for how trivial they sound and some question whether they are excessive complainers. One NT partner once said to me, 'You must think I am harping on about nothing. I am not one to complain but I feel that is all I do because nothing ever changes. There is no learning and no one seems to understand what I am talking about.' This is typical of how it can feel for the NT partner, who will have a history of not being believed when they know all too well that what they are describing is true. Even if the NT partner is aware that their partner is affected by Asperger syndrome, and as such not deliberately causing this emotional deprivation, this will not prevent CADD. Sometimes this knowledge can make it harder for the NT partner as they will feel guilt for knowing the AS partner cannot give the emotional support needed. The AS partner cannot give the emotional reciprocity their partner needs simply because they are unable to do so. This is why I emphasise a strategy of no blame.

What causes CADD?

The easiest way to understand CADD is to relate it to seasonal affective disorder (SAD). SAD is caused by sunlight deprivation, which can create a neurochemical imbalance in the brain. This can result in sleep problems, lethargy, overeating, depression, loss of self-esteem, hopelessness, social problems and a desire to avoid social contact, anxiety, tension, a loss of libido, mood changes and signs of a weakened immune system. SAD is very real. However, where SAD is about sunlight deprivation, CADD is about emotional deprivation. The CADD sufferer experiences similar symptoms to those of the SAD sufferer. But there is a more damaging effect upon the CADD sufferer insofar as it is another human being whom they probably love who is responsible, usually unintentionally, for their emotional deprivation – this can be a partner or a parent.

The fact that it is unintentional is only realised when the reason for the behaviour is discovered either by self-diagnosis or diagnosis by a professional. Living in a relationship where Asperger syndrome is undiagnosed or denied will often result in the NT person being blamed for the problems in the relationship by their partner, family, friends and society. In society it is often the very people who should be supporting the NT partners and their families who let them down – doctors, counsellors, therapists, teachers or psychologists – all through a lack of awareness of Asperger syndrome and its effects. They choose not to believe the NT person and view them as the one with the problem. The effects of CADD are likely to be at their height when the NT person (male or female) finds themselves in the position of not being believed by the AS person, friends, family and professionals.

These feelings of confusion, aloneness, desperation and not being believed have resulted in the name Cassandra being applied to the condition. My research, drawn from all over the world, based upon a questionnaire study that extends over the last ten years, strongly indicates that CADD develops as a consequence of being in an intimate relationship with an adult with Asperger syndrome. The AS person's inability to offer emotional reciprocity to their partner, children or family is the prime contributor to CADD.

Neurologically this inability to reciprocate emotionally is caused by alexithymia and lack of theory of mind. Alexithymia is a Greek term that literally means without words for feelings (Parker, Taylor and Bagby 2001). It has been found that 85 per cent of people with an autistic spectrum disorder are alexithymic (Hill *et al.* 2004). This can cause difficulties in expressing feelings. Add lack of theory of mind and there are further hindrances to these expressions (Beaumont and Newcombe 2006). As I have said, theory of mind is the ability to relate emotionally to another's mind state and be able to understand and appreciate their perception as being different to their own.

What are the symptoms of CADD?

Emotional health

- Low self-esteem.

- Feeling confused/bewildered.

- Feelings of anger.

- Feelings of guilt.

- Loss of self-identity.

Mental health

- Anger turns to depression.

- Anxiety.

- Phobias/social agoraphobia.

- Asperger ways.

- Complete breakdown.

Physical health

- Migraines.

- Loss or gain in weight.

- Premenstrual tension (PMT)/female-related problems.

- Low immune system – colds to cancer.

What can be done to prevent CADD?

Awareness and understanding are paramount in eliminating the condition. As CADD is a consequence of the situation a sufferer is in, it is therefore possible to find ways to alter that situation. Some relationships where one partner has AS can succeed if both partners understand their differences and work on developing a better or different way of communicating. I advise that this is undertaken with a therapist who has an understanding of CADD. If that is not possible then the couple or family can use some of the strategies offered in this book.

The effects of CADD can be reduced if both partners accept and understand why it occurs in the first place. This is unlikely to happen if there has been no diagnosis or acceptance that Asperger syndrome exists in a partner. Realisation that the problems in the relationship are the consequence of the differences between their respective emotional and physical needs can be the first step to recovery. Diagnosis by a professional or by oneself can offer answers to many questions, unexplained events or situations that have occurred in the relationship. It offers a reason for the breakdowns in communication, the embarrassing moments or avoidance of social situations. Most of all it tells both partners that neither is going mad and neither is to blame for the difficulties they have experienced.

The acceptance of Asperger syndrome can be the beginning of a new type of relationship. By developing understanding of the different way each processes information, good communication can begin. Using strategies such as those supplied in this workbook, reading the experiences of other couples affected by Asperger syndrome, looking at the research available and finding a therapist who is able to offer understanding to both partners will help the couple develop a better understanding of each other.

CADD is about deprivation. It is about a lack of emotional reciprocity which should be seen as a type of food that is crucial to the emotional survival of the NT partner which, if not received, will see self-esteem, self-confidence and self-identity damaged. The NT partner simply needs feeding and as this cannot be provided by the AS partner it will have to be found elsewhere. This does not mean there is nothing the AS partner can do. If their partner is feeling emotionally fed and content, then all will benefit. I have provided a list for both partners to consider and discuss together as to what is applicable to them and what might be practicably put into action.

Instructions for Preventing CADD lists

1   Find some time when you can discuss together and not be disturbed.

2   Both look at your appropriate list and tick the ones that you would like to do or are already doing.

3   Discuss these together as to how you might fit them in.

4   Use the blank sheets to fill in your own list.

5   Put them up on the wall in a prominent position so they will be noticed every day.

Preventing CADD – for the NT partner

	Tick
Meet up with friend/s.	
Join a gym.	
Take up a creative pastime.	
Join a ramblers/running club.	
Join an internet support group.	
Learn to pamper yourself, e.g. hairdresser/pedicure/massage.	
Have a coffee morning.	
Make use of your spiritual/religious group for support.	
Spoil yourself with something nice.	
Keep a feelings journal/diary.	

Preventing CADD – for the AS partner

	Tick
Give your partner a kiss when you are leaving the house.	
Greet your partner when you get home.	
Greet your partner when they arrive home.	
Say one nice thing to your partner every day.	
If your partner is upset, ask if they would like a hug.	
Give your partner a hug before you go to sleep.	
Hold your partner's hand when you are walking together.	
Ask your partner what sort of day they have had.	
Remember to call home if you are going to be late.	
Tell your partner you love them, even if you have said it before.	
Keep a feelings journal/diary.	
Send your partner a nice text message.	
Leave a post-it note for your partner to find with a nice message.	

Preventing CADD – for the NT partner

	Tick

Preventing CADD – for the AS partner

	Tick

Once again it is about trial and error, but if the incentive, motivation and commitment of the couple to make their relationship work are there, then by accepting and understanding the differences, *difference can work*. It will always be difficult. There are no miracle cures. It is about focusing on the positives and working through the negatives. It will invariably be the NT partner who will feel they are putting in the most effort, as it is the NT partner who is more able to be flexible and make changes. The NT partner will be learning to manage in an Asperger world. They will only be able to do this if they accept that there are some things their AS partner will never be able to provide which they will have to look for elsewhere or through other means.

For some couples, whatever they do, the relationship will not work and therefore the decision has to be made as to whether they stay in the relationship or not. Harsh as this may sound, it is sometimes the reality. However, I do say to the NT partner that if they are planning to end the relationship, do so because of who their partner is and not because of Asperger syndrome. Asperger syndrome affects all personality types. If someone is incompatible with someone else, they will still be incompatible whether they have Asperger syndrome or not.

Asperger syndrome brings positives and negatives to a relationship. Some couples are able to work with the negatives, accepting the difference and continuing to love one another. If the AS partner is in denial of their condition, they will more than likely blame their NT partner for all the problems in the relationship. If either of these is present in the relationship, then decisions need to be made as to how the relationship goes forward. Again, seeking out an appropriate therapist may be worthwhile in order for the couple to decide whether the relationship is at an end.

Chapter
Ten

DIFFERENCE CAN WORK

Discovery of Asperger syndrome offers a couple many choices. If the choice is for both to work at improving the relationship, with or without a therapist, then difference can work. It may take time and sometimes it will feel as if it is all uphill, but with enough love and commitment both can help each other over the rocky bits. The AS partner's capacity to logically work out how to climb over the rocks and the NT partner's emotional adeptness to help guide them in the darkness will make the couple strong allies.

I end with two emails sent to me by a couple that I performed an assessment with. The female partner also attended one of my workshops. They have given permission for their names to be published in this book. The first email is from Mark and the second from his wife Sennur. I believe they portray splendidly just how difference can work, with the right balance between acceptance and understanding of Asperger syndrome, and enough motivation, commitment and most of all the love that they share for each other.

My relationships did not last more than a year, before my partner would leave me usually with another man... The usual complaint was that I was not affectionate, and unable to talk, and did not understand the difference with sex and love. My response would be next girl I will adjust my behavior to correct the reason why she left, the problem would be that people are different and what might have worked with the last will not work with the present; I would use drugs and alcohol to deal with my problems.

I fell madly in love with my wife and decided to marry her the night we met. We rushed into marriage and, when my relationship problems started to surface she took the words until death do us part literally and stayed around. We had our ups and downs and children, but we always fought over the same things. I lied and eventually started having on-line affairs and living a secret life. When found out we started counseling again to save our marriage I blamed my wife for making me act the way I did and she was the major problem with our marriage. We spent a year going to counseling with no success and sessions ending in shouting matches and threats of divorce. Our incompetent counselor did not realize that I was incapable of understanding and I was an expert at seeing only what I wanted. The counselor started to have feelings for me and I was able to make her think my wife was the real problem. When we have talked about our sessions it seems that we had a different counselor and had a different session. In her frustration with me and her determination to try everything to save us, my wife learned about Aspergers and thought I had the symptoms. I did not believe her but I could not turn down a trip to England. I was nervous about meeting Maxine and the way she tested me and told me I had Aspergers I felt a relief. It was over and I no longer had to hide from others.

After getting diagnosed it all makes sense now, and I have realized that I was the major problem with our marriage, and I have become better with people.

I'm still semi detached from everyday emotions and still get wrapped up in the things that I think that are important to me, work computers, photography, non humane things that I can control. But I now realize that I can trust my wife and share things with her. We still have arguments at times and she knows that I don't act the way I'm on purpose but it's the way I'm wired. My thought process is still mostly reactive to things, if situation A comes up I'm suppose to do B, but some times I should have done C instead, that's when I get frustrated when I miss read situations. Not as much as before being diagnosed.

The most important thing since being diagnosed is that I can see the hell I have put my wife through and I'm amazed that she is the only one who has stayed around for me and I will try to overcome my inability to process feelings, and try to make her understand that I love her but sometimes it is hard for me to convey it. (Mark A. Simonson, USA)

On the day I was sure my husband [indeed] had Aspergers, I was able to move beyond anger, depression and negatively infested standstill emotion, I had been stuck in for so many years, as now, it had a name: Asperger syndrome. In my thirst for knowledge I ordered almost all of the books published on the subject. I discovered people and organizations online and, in the process, discovered Maxine Aston. What a discovery that was, I felt human, I felt validated, for the first time in a very long time, I discovered that the world of Aspergers didn't have to eat us alive. I set a course to make things work for us...

Professionally I am well versed in various areas, one of them is languages, another is customer service and public relations and, since I wasn't doing a brilliant job as a wife, as I was too emotionally involved, I decided to tackle it as if a consultant to myself. I started banking happy moments with my husband every single day. I made sure we had at least one positive exchange each day and, no matter what he did or said, I did not react. Reducing my reactions to his actions, left him without the ability to justify the bad things he was doing. I just kept reading and learning, attending conferences and workshops and implementing solutions in tiny steps. Instead of fighting his addictive personality I encouraged and guided him into photography, created gardens he could sit and enjoy, while he smoked his cigarettes and took pictures of said.

After confirming what I was doing was correct at a Cassandra Workshop in London with Maxine, I returned to England with my husband and youngest son in tow, to meet with Maxine again. Once my husband was diagnosed he actually accepted it and seemed at ease with it. A question he asked Maxine was, 'How do I know how to judge things at times?' To which she responded, 'When in doubt, ask Sennur, she knows.' No one had ever said that to my husband until then and I knew a page in our lives had turned. We had a fantastic trip in England and when we returned home we had a new purpose in our life.

The monster was out of the closet and it was not scary. I was a woman with a mission, with a lot at stake and it was up to me set the course. I finally had my husband's commitment to our marriage, he was going to follow and share the responsibilities. At first we relaxed, basking in the knowledge, letting it sink in, just enjoying each other's company.

We had to learn to communicate more effectively, I learned to ask more specific questions that I knew my husband would respond to more positively and he learned to trust me enough to answer them truthfully. Additionally I had to learn not to expect!! Such a hard thing for a woman, how could one not have expectations? I

134 • *The Asperger Couple's Workbook*

simply told my husband what I would like and how I would like it to be done. This kind of clarity helped our relationship. In the end it was about communication and the style in which we communicated with each other. I understood this well, we spoke different languages and by making an effort to communicate each time, we achieved clearer communication.

If my husband isn't able to do something, he simply says: 'I don't understand this, I am "Aspergic", and could you explain this please?' He explains it's the way he is wired and that he processes things differently to them. If I tell him what we are doing and when he needs to be out the door, 99% of the time he is there, ready to go, waiting for me in his wrinkled clothes, if I hadn't told him what to wear. Then I realize I forgot to give him the dress code. We've both learned to check our egos at the door and stop keeping score. It is no longer about who did what to whom. It is about us and our relationship. Clear and concise communication is in every part of our lives now. We practice it religiously. We do things with goodwill and no longer judge negatively.

My husband appreciates me now, he tells me so, he does things to make my life better and in return I try to make his better too. Aspergers is woven into the fabric of our lives and we are who we are because of it. We wouldn't have it any other way as we have grown together with it and become better people for it. After 20 years of marriage we are actually looking to the future, to having a lot of great times together. Recently we renewed our vows in Pubol, Spain, in front of the castle Salvador Dali gave his wife Gala. I stood there, listening to my husband tell me how much he loves me, appreciates me and is so grateful for everything I have done, to save our marriage. As he held both my hands, gently caressing them, my husband thanked me for being who I am and asked me to never change. All I could say was 'I love you' – I didn't need to utter anything else, he finally knew my heart. (Sennur Fahrali)

REFERENCES

Aston, M. (2001) *The Other Half of Asperger Syndrome.* London: National Autistic Society.

Aston, M. (2003) 'Autism through the Ages.' Paper presented to the FAAAS Conference, Boston, Massachusetts, 9–10 May 2003.

Aston, M. (2007) 'The Effects upon Mental and Physical Health when Living in a Relationship where One Partner has Asperger Syndrome.' Paper presented to the Congress Autisme in Het Gezin, Zuidlaren, The Netherlands, 1 November 2007.

Attwood, T. (1998) *Asperger's Syndrome: A Guide for Parents and Professionals.* London: Jessica Kingsley Publishers.

Attwood, T. (2007) *The Complete Guide to Asperger's Syndrome.* London: Jessica Kingsley Publishers.

Beaumont, R. and Newcombe, P. (2006) 'Theory of mind and central coherence in adults with high-functioning autism or Asperger syndrome.' *Autism: The International Journal of Research and Practice 10,* 4, 365–382.

Carter, R. (1998) *Mapping the Mind.* London: Weidenfeld and Nicolson.

Happe, F. and Frith, U. (1995) 'Theory of Mind in Autism.' In E. Schopler and G.B. Mesibov (eds) *Learning and Cognition in Autism.* New York: Plenum Press.

Hill, E., Berthoz, S. and Frith, U. (2004) 'Brief report: cognitive processing of own emotions in individuals with autistic spectrum disorder and in their relatives.' *Journal of Autism and Developmental Disorders 34,* 2, 229–235.

Holliday Willey, L. and Attwood, T. (2000) *Asperger's Syndrome – Crossing the Bridge.* London: Jessica Kingsley Publishers..

Lawson, W. (2005) *Sex, Sexuality and the Autistic Spectrum.* London: Jessica Kingsley Publishers.

Ozonoff, S., Roger, S.J. and Pennington, B.F. (1991) 'Asperger's syndrome: evidence of an empirical distinction from high-functioning autism.' *Journal of Child Psychology and Psychiatry 32,* 1107–22.

Parker, J.D.A., Taylor, G.J. and Bagby, R.M. (2001) 'The relationship between emotional intelligence and alexithymia.' *Journal of Personality and Individual Differences 30,* 107–115.

Rodman, K. (2003) *Aspergers syndrome and Adults... Is Anyone Listening? Essays and Poems by Spouses, Partners and Parents of Adults with Asperger Syndrome.* London: Jessica Kingsley Publishers.

Thompson, J. (2008) *Emotionally Dumb: An Introduction to Alexithymia.* London: Jessica Kingsley Publishers.

FURTHER READING

Aston, M. (2003a) 'Asperger syndrome in the counselling room.' *Counselling and Psychotherapy Journal 14*, 5, 10–12.

Aston, M. (2003b) *Aspergers in Love*. London: Jessica Kingsley Publishers.

Aston, M. (2005) 'Growing up in an Asperger family.' *Counselling Children and Young People*. Summer, 6–9.

Aston, M. (2007) *Recognising AS and its Implications for Therapy*. BACP information sheet G9. Lutterworth: BACP.

Bentley, K. (2007) *Alone Together: Making an Asperger Marriage Work*. London: Jessica Kingsley Publishers.

Hénault, I. (2006) *Asperger's Syndrome and Sexuality: From Adolescence through Adulthood*. London: Jessica Kingsley Publishers.

Hendrickx, S. (2008) *Love, Sex and Long-Term Relationships*. London: Jessica Kingsley Publishers.

Hendrickx, S. and Newton, K. (2007) *Asperger Syndrome – A Love Story*. London: Jessica Kingsley Publishers.

Holliday Willey, L. (1999) *Pretending to Be Normal*. London: Jessica Kingsley Publishers.

Holliday Willey, L. (2001) *Asperger's Syndrome in the Family*. London: Jessica Kingsley Publishers.

Jackson, L. (2002) *Freaks, Geeks and Asperger's Syndrome*. London: Jessica Kingsley Publishers.

Slater-Walker, G. and Slater-Walker, C. (2002) *An Asperger Marriage*. London: Jessica Kingsley Publishers.

Tinsley, M. and Hendrickx, S. (2008) *Asperger Syndrome and Alcohol: Drinking to Cope?* London: Jessica Kingsley Publishers.

FURTHER INFORMATION AND RESEARCH

For more information on Maxine's work and to participate in her current research visit www.maxineaston.co.uk

INDEX

Note: the letter 'i' after a page number refers to an illustration; the letter 'w' refers to a worksheet.

Author Index